844

(3203)

ROBERT M. LA FOLLETTE, JR.

ROBERT M. LA FOLLETTE, JR.

and the decline of the

PROGRESSIVE PARTY IN WISCONSIN

by

Roger T. Johnson

Archon Books
1970

First published 1964 by
The State Historical Society of Wisconsin
Reprinted 1970 with permission
in an unaltered and unabridged edition

ISBN: 0 208 00847 0
Library of Congress Catalog Card Number: 70- 113017
Printed in the United States of America

ISBN: 0 208 00847 0
Library of Congress Catalog Card Number: 70- 113017
Printed in the United States of America

To my

Mother and Father

PREFACE

Robert Marion La Follette, Jr. would not have liked the emphasis this book places on his career. He entered politics only because he was the son of a prominent public figure, and was thrust into the Senate upon his father's death in 1925. Over the years he became recognized as a man of ability and integrity, and he established a reputation as a conscientious public servant, as a legislative craftsman. He was quite proud of the record he made in Congress. This book does not cover La Follette's role as a United States Senator, nor is it a history of the Wisconsin Progressives during this period; rather, it studies Robert M. La Follette, Jr. as a political leader when the Progressive movement founded by his father was in its decline.

Many persons have aided me in the preparation of this book, and I wish to express my appreciation to them. Mr. John Steinke of the University of Wisconsin very generously made available to me correspondence from his personal files relevant to the 1946 campaign, for which I am heavily indebted. Professor David A. Shannon of the University of Wisconsin read the manuscript in its entirety and offered countless helpful suggestions. My friend, Miss Linda Rieke, helped me in the time-consuming task of proof-reading, and caught many grammatical absurdities which otherwise would have remained in the book.

Madison, Wisconsin   *Roger T. Johnson*
January, 1964

vii

CONTENTS

Chapter I

YOUNG BOB

On June 18, 1925, Robert Marion La Follette died. For twenty-five years he had dominated Wisconsin politics. Three times he had been elected Governor of the state and, in 1906, he went to the United States Senate, where he served for nineteen years. He became and he remained a national figure. Controversy followed him throughout his life; it was impossible to be neutral about Robert M. La Follette. "Few men of his generation have been so loved," Bruce Bliven wrote. "No man of his generation has been more hated."[1]

The rapid industrialization of the United States during the last half of the nineteenth century had produced new social, economic and political tensions. Many Americans, yearning for the supposed purity of the pre-industrial United States, were disturbed by the vast changes which the new industrialization had wrought upon American society; La Follette was one of these. He called himself a Progressive, and joined the fight against the evils of the new industrial order. He brought to this battle an extraordinarily energetic and dominating personality. The use of governmental power to reduce the concentration of industrial and financial power, the regulation of railroads, the income tax, the direct primary—these were cardinal principles in the La Follette creed.

Senator La Follette opposed America's entry into the Great War, for he believed that the war did not affect the vital interests of the United States. More than that, he feared that the efforts involved in waging the war would sap much of the

1

energy necessary to the success of the progressive movement
for domestic reform.   The fervor of patriotic intensity and his
own actions caused extreme denunciations of treason and pro-
Germanism to be cast upon him.   Senator La Follette survived
the war;   he went on to achieve his greatest electoral triumph
when Wisconsin overwhelmingly re-elected him to the Senate
in 1922.

After the Great War, however, La Follette worked on a political soil less fertile than it had been two decades before.
America had acquiesced in the triumph of industrialization and,
it seemed, in the rule of the businessman as well. La Follette
continued the fight for his progressive principles in a nation
which seemed to care less for progressive principles than ever
before.   In 1924, at the age of sixty-nine, Senator La Follette,
who had always run under the Republican banner, left the party
altogether to lead an independent ticket as a candidate for
President.   He chose Senator Burton K. Wheeler, a Montana
Democrat and a Progressive, as his running-mate.   President
Calvin Coolidge and the Democratic nominee, John W. Davis,
ignored each other and directed most of their verbal fire against
La Follette. Senator La Follette did not expect to win; he made
the race as a matter of principle, and as a matter of practical
politics, hoping that a strong showing would generate the popular support necessary to the formation of a new national party.
This, however, did not happen.   President Coolidge won with
15,275,003 votes; Davis finished second with 8,385,586 votes,
and La Follette ran a distant third with 4,826,471 votes, approximately sixteen per cent of the total.   He carried but one
state, ever-loyal Wisconsin. In the aftermath of the campaign
his health steadily declined, and on June 18, 1925, just four
days after his seventieth birthday, he died.

La Follette was returned to his home town, Madison, Wisconsin.   Forty thousand people passed by his body as it lay
in the rotunda of the state capitol.   "Upon few men has Wisconsin bestowed higher honors in life and perhaps to none has
she given so impressive a tribute in death," a *New York Times*
news story said.   "Yet there was nothing of pomp or display.
It was the outpouring of peoples, high and low, bowing their
heads in silent respect."[2] Before the end of June the Wisconsin Legislature unanimously chose La Follette as one of the

state's two representatives in the Hall of Fame of the United States capitol. In such a time of mourning it seemed inappropriate and indecent to consider matters of politics. Yet, La Follette's death had removed Wisconsin's senior Senator and the undisputed master of the state's dominant political faction. One question could not long remain unanswered: who would replace him?

La Follette had played two roles, United States Senator and state political leader. The most immediate political problem was his Senate seat. According to Wisconsin law, the Governor was to call a special election to fill a vacant office. In such an election a Republican victory was assured. Wisconsin had always been a one-party state, and Republican predominance reached new heights in the 1920's. Yet, in the actual terms of political combat, Wisconsin had all the markings of a two-party state. The Republicans were split into two irreconcilable factions, the Progressives and the Stalwarts. Each faction had its own separate organization. For each faction the Republican primary was the final and decisive battle; the winner found the general election merely a formality, for the Wisconsin Democrats were but an insignificant political force. The Progressives usually prevailed, but occasionally Stalwarts would win. Senator Irvine Lenroot, once a La Follette man himself, was the recognized leader of the Stalwarts, and he had faced strenuous opposition from Senator La Follette when he won re-election in 1920.

The Progressives, however, faced a split in their own ranks. While he had lived Senator La Follette ruled the Progressive organization with an iron hand. He could say who was and was not Progressive and usually make it stick. None in the ranks spoke out against La Follette; all gave one hundred per cent public support to the Progressive leader. The long years of La Follette domination of the Progressive organization, however, had begun to produce some bitterness within the ranks, bitterness which was never publicly expressed but which existed nonetheless. After La Follette's death few eulogized him more eloquently than Representative Henry Allen Cooper. Privately, however, Cooper showed his bitterness at the long La Follette domination. "I was never devoted to La Follette," Cooper lamented. "Had I been 'devoted' to him, and ready always to follow, I would long ago have been in the Senate. He & his machine followers twice deliberately defeated me for the Senate because I do my own thinking."[3]

Governor John J. Blaine was the focal point for the dissension in the Progressive ranks. In 1924 he had supported the La Follette presidential campaign and La Follette had supported him for a third term. A dissident group of Progressives, known as the "Progressive insurgents," opposed Blaine's renomination in the Republican primary. These anti-Blaine Progressives included Secretary of State Fred R. Zimmerman (who later nearly made this office hereditary), and E. J. Gross, President of the La Follette Progressive Association. They supported Lieutenant Governor George F. Comings for Governor; Comings claimed that he was "the only candidate for governor who during this campaign has ben [*sic*] preaching pure and undefiled La Follette progressive principles."[4] Bob La Follette recognized the potential dangers in a Progressive split when, in his statement of support for Governor Blaine, he repeatedly pointed out the dangers of a break in the Progressive ranks: "It would be nothing short of a tragedy if, through disagreement over candidates or through differences in respect to policy, the Progressives of Wisconsin should permit the reactionary, predatory forces within the state to return to power at a time when the whole nation is looking to Wisconsin for leadership. . . . Any break in our ranks will but serve to strengthen those forces against which we are contending. . . . Let us not be guilty of dividing our forces in the face of a crafty and united foe."[5] In the primary Blaine buried Comings in an avalanche of votes; still, the Progressive insurgents were not reconciled to the Governor. All Progressives, however, publicly united upon their devotion to Old Bob La Follette; the mutterings and bitterness against him never approached the point of an open revolt. Comings claimed that he was true to the Progressivism of La Follette but that Blaine really was not. Blaine countered that his devotion to La Follette progressivism was second to none. La Follette seemed to be the sole factor holding the Wisconsin Progressives together; without him, it seemed possible that the movement would fragment.

Further complicating the Progressives' position was an apparent resurgence among the Stalwarts. The Stalwarts, who regarded Calvin Coolidge as their national leader, had their tolerance for Old Bob La Follette stretched far beyond the breaking point when, in 1924, he maintained his stranglehold on the Wisconsin Republican party but ran on an independent ticket against the Republican President. It was time, the Stalwarts thought, that the Wisconsin Republican party be given back to the Republicans. Hence, in the spring of 1925, just a few months before La Follette's death, the Stalwarts organized the Republican Voluntary Committee; this was an attempt to organize more effectively the non-Progressive and anti-La Follette elements of the Wisconsin Republican party. The new Voluntary Committee displayed an optimism and an enthusiasm which gave at least a little concern to the Progressive leaders, compounding their problems of threatened disunity within their own ranks.

Now that La Follette was dead, an abundance of Progressive politicians could come forth, each claiming that he should be the humble heir to the great leader's place in the Senate. The potency of La Follette's blessing had served as a restraining hand on the ambitions of other Progressives while he lived; now that he was gone, and gone with him was the potency of his blessing, the danger loomed very large that his organization would split into many fragments. Governor Blaine, Secretary of State Zimmerman, and Congressmen Cooper, John Mandt Nelson and John Schafer all flirted with the idea of running in the special election. In the days after La Follette's death reports circulated that his personal choice would have been altogether different. "Could La Follette have done such a thing," one reporter noted, "he would almost certainly have designated Attorney General [Herman L.] Ekern as his heir apparent. No one was politically closer to 'Fighting Bob.'"[6] "Herman Ekern . . . would ordinarily, it is thought, be the choice of Senator La Follette to succeed him," another news story said.[7] But La Follette had indicated no preference, and now he could not step in and say which one of these pretenders should carry the torch of Progressivism. Obviously, more than one Progressive candidate could split the Progressive vote so dramatically as to pave the way for a Stalwart victory. Nothing else could be such a sacrilege to Old Bob's memory; more than that, it might ring down the curtain on the Progressives as an

effective political force in Wisconsin. Blaine could claim that
he was more of a La Follette Progressive than Zimmerman, and
Zimmerman could claim that he was more of a La Follette Progressive than Blaine or Representative Cooper, and Cooper
could claim that he was more of a La Follette Progressive than
anyone else.   But no one could claim that he was more of a
La Follette Progressive than a La Follette. Progressives of all
factions came to realize that a member of the La Follette family, more than any other candidate, would bring unity to the
Progressive ranks.   But which La Follette?   Old Bob had an
able and industrious wife and two sons.

    At first, attention focused on the Senator's widow, Belle
Case La Follette. She would surely unite the Progressives and
ride the crest of a wave of sentimentality; moreover, she would
draw support from other sectors to assure her triumph. A group
of prominent Wisconsin women saw an opportunity to advance
the feminist cause by electing her to the Senate. "Let us give
her our backing," they said.   "She needs our assurance that
she is wanted."[8]   Furthermore, the Stalwarts might even decline the hopeless task of opposing the Senator's widow. They
realized that Mrs. La Follette was over sixty years old and
that she could not long remain in the Senate; after three years
she probably would retire, and that might open the way for a
Stalwart victory.   But Mrs. La Follette simply did not want to
run.   She had never enjoyed political combat, and, now that
her husband was dead, she would enjoy it even less. Despite
tremendous pressure she remained adamant in her refusal to
make the race.

    With Mrs. La Follette out of consideration, attention then
focused on her two sons. Her younger son, Philip Fox La Follette, was the logical family heir to his father's political career; no one doubted this.   "Young Phil La Follette was supposed to be the one of the flock who embodied the qualities
to make him the logical successor to his father," a feature
article on the La Follette family said.   "not only the family
but the followers of La Follette [singled Phil] out as his father's likely successor."[9] He had a natural interest in politics
and ability as a speaker, having campaigned extensively in
his father's behalf in 1924.   In that year he was elected District Attorney of Dane County, the position in which his father

had begun his political career back in 1880. The parallel between father and son seemed clear. Yet, one insurmountable barrier blocked Phil La Follette's path in 1925: he was only twenty-eight years old, two years under the constitutional requirement for a United States Senator. Had he been at least thirty years old, there is little doubt that he would have been the La Follette candidate and the Progressive candidate for his father's Senate seat. His older and less politically inclined brother was barely thirty, just meeting the constitutional requirement. Because of the necessity of a La Follette, because of Mrs. La Follette's refusal to run and Phil La Follette's inability to run, Robert M. La Follette, Jr. loomed as the Progressives' most desirable candidate.

Robert M. La Follette, Jr. was born on February 6, 1895, and grew up in a political environment. "Young Bob" entered the University of Wisconsin in the fall of 1913, but illness forced him to withdraw a year and a half later. He re-entered the University, but illness again compelled him to leave in February, 1917. For nine months in 1918, when his father's political career had reached its nadir, Young Bob lay near death. Throughout the rest of his life ill health constantly plagued him. In 1919, recovered and as healthy as he would ever be, he became his father's secretary, serving as one of his closest political advisers for the next six years. Young Bob La Follette managed the Progressive campaign in 1922, and in that year he became the chairman of the Republican state central committee, a position he still held in 1925. In the 1924 Presidential campaign he served as his father's personal manager, working quietly behind the scenes.

Young Bob was a shy, quiet individual, one who did not want to impose himself on others, one who preferred to remain in the background. Politics was thrust upon him; were he not the son of a prominent politician he never would have chosen public life as a career. Left to his own devices he might have chosen commerce, or banking, or journalism, but he certainly would not have chosen politics. A few months before Old Bob La Follette died, a journalist wrote that "Anyone acquainted with [Young Bob] La Follette knows it is his desire to get out of politics, even as his father's secretary, and that it is only his sense of filial duty that keeps him at that task."[10] Unlike

his more out-going and volatile younger brother, who by 1925
had spoken to countless political rallies, Young Bob had given
only one public speech in his career; in the summer of 1924 he
read his father's statement to the Cleveland Progressive Convention. Despite his quiet and unassuming nature and his relative disinterest in politics, Young Bob was thirty years old
and clearly available and, more than anyone else, he could
unite the Progressives. *The Nation* looked apprehensively at
Old Bob's empty shoes, but then it became unbounded in its
enthusiasm for Young Bob's ability to fill them:

> Prodigiously energetic, unfalteringly enthusiastic,
> sound in reasoning yet quick in decision, always un-
> assuming, he managed somehow to keep together a
> host of heterogeneous and disparate elements [in the
> 1924 campaign.] His cheerfulness was a constant
> inspiration to every campaign worker. If any man pos-
> sesses the qualities of leadership it is thirty-year
> old Bob La Follette. His father entered Congress
> even younger, and few Senators after a whole term in
> office know Washington's problems and pitfalls as
> well as he. None other in the Progressive group of
> Wisconsin could speak both for the State and for the
> nation as effectively.[11]

Most Progressives clearly wanted Robert M. La Follette, Jr.
to run for the Senate.

On July 29 Governor Blaine called a special election to
fill the vacant Senate seat; the primary was to be held on September 15 and the election would follow two weeks later. The
next day, after a series of conferences with Progressive leaders, Young Bob La Follette said simply: "I am a candidate
for United States senator. In a short time I shall issue a complete statement."[12]

La Follette's announcement did not immediately unite all
Progressives behind his candidacy. His brother-in-law, Ralph
Sucher, sought support for him by urging the necessity of Progressive unity. "Doubtless you also have an opinion," Sucher
wrote to one Progressive, "as to whether the Progressive movement nationally would be best served by the election of Mr.
La Follette or by the election of a 'regular, [*sic*] whose vic-

tory would be heralded to the country as proof that the movement in Wisconsin was built on personal idolatry and was
doomed to collapse at the Senator's death."[13] Young Bob himself used the same appeal: "The reactionaries realize that a
victory for a reactionary or a near Progressive—it makes no
difference which—would be heralded all over the country as
a repudiation by Wisconsin of Progressive principles to which
Robert M. La Follette devoted his life."[14] Many anti-Blaine
Progressives, particularly a group in the state Senate and Congressmen Cooper, Nelson, and Schafer, were apprehensive at
the possibility of a La Follette-Blaine alliance; they viewed
with alarm the recent conferences between the two men. They
feared that Young Bob was making a deal for Blaine's support
in the special election in exchange for La Follette's support
for the Governor if he challenged Senator Lenroot in 1926.
(This is, in fact, precisely what did happen.) For this reason
Congressmen Cooper and Schafer considered running against
La Follette. In the middle of August La Follette made his peace
with the Progressive Congressmen. The terms of the pact revealed the Congressmen's dislike for Blaine, and their dislike
for the one-man domination of the Progressive organization in
the last years of Old Bob's life. Young Bob guaranteed the
group that he had made "no entangling alliances" with Blaine,
and agreed that he would not attempt to boss the Congressional
delegation but would confer with it on matters of policy and on
the choice of candidates. In reporting on this meeting Congressman Nelson, who had run the 1924 La Follette presidential campaign, commented: "We submitted to his father's leadership, but we would not stand for any boss or ring here-
after."[15] After this meeting the anti-Blaine Congressmen came
out, one by one, and announced their support for Young Bob.

Robert M. La Follette, Jr., then, was the only available
candidate who could unite the Progressives; even then, he did
not have an easy time of it. In the campaign which followed,
Young Bob announced that he was running on his father's platform of 1922. He went on to say:

> I do not ask the support of the people of Wiscon-
> sin because I am Robert M. La Follette's son. I am
> well aware that this relationship in itself does not

entitle my candidacy to consideration. At the same
time that relationship does not disqualify me.

La Follette then filled in the details of his platform. He favored the direct nomination and election of the President. He
favored governmental operation of the Muscle Shoals power
plant. He favored the repeal of the Esch-Cummins Railroad
Law of 1920. He favored reduced freight rates on agricultural
products. He favored the strengthening of the Federal Trade
Commission. He opposed any unjust use of the injunction in
labor disputes. He opposed the Mellon tax plan. He opposed
imperialism. And, he opposed American entry into the World
Court as merely back door entry to the League of Nations. All
in all, this was a fairly standard statement of the position of
middlewestern Progressives in the 1920's. La Follette concluded his statement with the ringing declaration:

> The great honor and privilege of completing my
> father's unexpired term entail tremendous obligations
> which I would undertake with a deep sense of re-
> sponsibility and a determination to maintain the prin-
> ciples to which he dedicated his life. Upon the prin-
> ciples which were his guide to public service I take
> my stand. I shall not compromise and I will not sur-
> render.[16]

The Progressive leaders were apprehensive about Young
Bob's ability to campaign; he had never done it before. La Follette himself was doubtless apprehensive about his own prospects, and how he would fare on the hustings. One of his father's most trusted political lieutenants asked Young Bob what
he would do if he were heckled. A look of anxiety came across
his face. "I haven't the slightest idea," he said.[17] In contrast
to his father, who delivered each speech with all the fervor
and energy and all the conviction of an evangelist, Young Bob
developed a style far more even, far quieter, far less fiery.
His standard speech in 1925 was, in substance, very much
like a speech his father might have given, but he delivered it
in a noticeably straight-forward, unemotional manner.   The
story has often been told that he improved his delivery and
gained greater confidence after he lost the outline to the
speech.[18]

   Young Bob La Follette insisted that he was running on his
own, that he was asking the voters of Wisconsin to consider
him on his experience, his merits, and his platform. He con-
tinually repeated that his special relationship with the man
whose Senate seat he sought to fill did not qualify him for that
office. Yet, he left no doubt who his father was. In his standard speech he mentioned him by name eighteen times.

> I have always felt that the only thing that could
> match the devotion of Robert M. La Follette to the
> ideals of the Progressive movement was the devotion
> of the people of Wisconsin to those principles. So
> long as Robert M. La Follette was fighting for those
> principles, even if he fought alone, the people of
> this state stood back of him.

Young Bob used the same phrases, the same issues, and the
same attacks which had so long characterized his father's
career. "The great money power never sleeps," he said. "Its
supremacy depends on control of legislation, state and national."[19] In speaking to some railroad workers in Milwaukee,
La Follette said:

> I have a great desire and determination to keep up
> the good fight. In the many years of association with
> Robert M. La Follette I have been in close fellowship
> with representatives of labor at Washington and else-
> where in the country. I believe I have the right under-
> standing and the right purpose.[20]

Robert M. La Follette, Jr. campaigned as the son and political
heir of Robert M. La Follette.

   Despite the professions of confidence which the Progressives made and despite the sentimentality which doubtless
existed, Young Bob's triumph was not taken for granted. Altogether ten men (one Socialist, one Democrat, four Independ-
ents, and four Republicans) entered the race, a record number.
The Socialists, who had supported Senator La Follette when he
ran for the Senate in 1922 and when he ran for President in
1924, did not support his son in 1925. Socialist Congressman
Victor Berger explained: "I believe young Bobbie ought to take
time to earn his spurs. Furthermore, this is not an inherited

monarchy, expecially in Wisconsin.   Why should we have to
take a crown prince? "[21] The Socialist candidate for the Senate, John M. Work, claimed that he was the true heir to the
1924 La Follette Presidential candidacy:

> Voters of Wisconsin who followed La Follette out
> of the Republican party will not go back.   They will
> go forward, as La Follette himself always did.   That
> means they will vote the Socialist ticket.
>
> Since no new party was organized, the Socialist
> party is the logical and legitimate heir of the La Fol-
> lette movement of 1924.[22]

Work probably had no illusions of victory, but his candidacy
would drain some votes from La Follette.

The newly-organized Republican Voluntary Committee met
at Oshkosh and dubbed former state Senator Roy P. Wilcox as
the knight who would slay this silly notion that Young Bobbie
should go to the Senate.   In 1918 Wilcox had led the fight in
the state Senate to condemn Old Bob La Follette for his position on the war. The Voluntary Committee had hoped to present
a united front against Young Bob La Follette, but in this it
failed, for two other Republicans entered the primary.   Daniel
Woodward ran with the support of the Ku Klux Klan.   Former
Governor Francis McGovern (1911—1915), who had been a La
Follette Progressive until he fell out of Old Bob's favor in
1912, also entered the race. In 1925 McGovern spoke of Coolidge's "wise and prudent leadership," hardly the most Progressive of things to say.   However, when he got to the spe-
cifics of national issues, he usually agreed with La Follette;
this coupled with his record as a Progressive Governor indicated that McGovern probably would draw some support from
Young Bob.

Roy P. Wilcox emerged as La Follette's main primary opponent.   He campaigned on a pro-Coolidge and anti-Blaine
platform.   With the anti-Coolidge Progressives in control of
the Wisconsin Republican party, Wilcox's campaign sounded
the war-cry of "the Republican party for Republicans." "A new
deal in Wisconsin politics is demanded which shall be in
hearty accord with President Coolidge in his program for reduced taxation and efficient constitutional government," Wil-

cox said. "We are fortunate to have such a leader."[23] A vote for Wilcox, a newspaper ad proclaimed, was a vote to continue the "tried and proven" Coolidge policies, for Wilcox was the only candidate true enough to his Republican convictions to support the President in 1924.[24] Wilcox directed much of his attack upon the state administration of Governor Blaine, which the Stalwarts dubbed the "Madison ring," on the understandable assumption that this was the Progressives' weakest flank.

Senator Irvine Lenroot campaigned strenuously for Roy Wilcox. The Senator was clearly concerned with the "Madison ring," for the ringleader appeared to be a rather formidable threat to him in 1926. "There are just two issues in this campaign," Lenroot said. "Do you believe in President Coolidge? And, do you believe there ought to be a house cleaning at Madison?"[25] The Coolidge administration wanted an affirmative answer to both questions, and Republican National Chairman William M. Butler set about to produce it. "I wish you would take pains to deny as emphatically as you wish that I have ever had or have now any intention of supporting La Follette, Jr.," Butler wrote to a Wisconsin Republican. "On the other hand, I hope very much that a real republican candidate can be selected to run for senator in your state."[26] On the eve of the primary Chairman Butler repeated that "the republican national committee cannot support him [La Follette.]"[27] Only a few months before his death, Senator La Follette, along with Senators Ladd, Frazier, and Brookhart, had been declared *personae non gratae* by the Republican party for their support of the third party ticket in 1924; they were denied the committee posts to which their seniority as Republicans would have entitled them. Young Bob would be just about as unpalatable to the Republicans in Washington as Old Bob was.

Progressives throughout the nation who had come to look upon Wisconsin as a spiritual home flocked to the state to aid Young Bob La Follette. Senator George Norris, the conscience of national Progressivism, expressed no desire to suggest to Wisconsin voters who the proper candidate was, but he did suggest to them that the special election was very important for Progressives all over the nation. "I do not believe anyone who knows the conditions here as I think I do, no matter how he feels toward Mr. La Follette, Jr., will doubt for a moment his qualifications to take up the work where his father laid it down."[28] Senator Burton K. Wheeler of Montana said: "No man in the United States Senate knows the various members of the Senate better than Robert La Follette, Jr. There isn't a man in the Senate today who knows the actual processes of legislation better than Robert La Follette, Jr., and there isn't a man in the Senate today, in my opinion, who is better qualified by training, experience, or natural ability to sit in that body."[29] In a joint appearance in Madison, Congressmen Knud Welfald of Minnesota and Fiorello H. La Guardia of New York declared that from the farms of Minnesota to the tenements of New York all eyes were on the campaign in Wisconsin.[30] Andrew Furuseth of the Seaman's Union and William Green of the American Federation of Labor formally endorsed La Follette. Four railroad brotherhoods urged that Progressive voters must support Young Bob, "not because his name is La Follette, but because of the fact that the people of Wisconsin, knowing his Progressive principles, are convinced that he will take up and manfully bear the burden laid down by his illustrious father."[31] Finally, one observer whose poison barbs neglected few subjects in the 1920's, commented: "Young Bob, entering that charnel-house of once honorable men, would be worth a thousand of the usual cadavers. He would come in like a clear wind. He would bring his brilliant youngness with him, and an honorable name, and a tradition of high and unshakable character," H. L. Mencken said. "I hope he wins."[32]

Robert M. La Follette, Jr. was attracting the most interest and drawing the largest crowds, but some skeptics suggested that people were just curious to see how he was doing. Old Bob had never lost a state-wide race, but how well this vote-getting prowess could be transferred to his son remained in doubt. The September 15 primary provided the answer. The Wisconsin primary is unique. There is no party registration in the state; rather, at every primary the voter receives a separate ballot for each party. He may vote on only one of the ballots, and hence in the primary of only one party, but he is perfectly free to choose the party in which he will cast his primary vote. In this primary, of 332,435 total votes, 318,709 were cast in the Republican column. McGovern received 18,478 votes, Woodward received 40,366 votes, Wilcox re-

ceived 81,834 votes, and La Follette received an absolute majority, with 178,031 votes.   He failed to carry but seven of
Wisconsin's seventy-one counties. He lost Chippewa, Dunn,
and Pepin, three small, contiguous counties in the western part
of the state, to Woodward, and Rock, Walworth, Kenosha, and
Marinette counties to Wilcox.[33]   "Of the elder La Follette's
extraordinary personality,   political genius and continuous
power in his own state the result of Tuesday's primaries is
even more striking proof than the long years of his reign," *The
New York Times* said editorially.   "The dead hand and brain
are still mighty."[34] La Follette's victory statement paid glowing tribute to the triumph of his father's principles:

> Wisconsin has once more reaffirmed her faith in
> the fundamental principles of the Progressive cause
> to which Robert M. La Follette consecrated his life.
> In a campaign in which the issue was clear cut and
> simple between the forces of reaction and of progress,
> the voters of this State have given their answer to
> the country that they rededicate themselves to the
> movement for bringing government back to the peo-
> ple.[35]

As was the case in Wisconsin throughout the 1920's, the
primary proved to be the decisive battle.   La Follette won so
overwhelming a victory that the outcome of the special election was never really in doubt.   Yet the young candidate prepared to embark upon another campaign tour, explaining: "In
view of the fact that the progressive vote was a majority over
the combined votes of the opposition the spirit of over-confi-
dence must not develop."[36]   *The New York Times* observed
that "unless all signs fail, Robert M. La Follette, Jr. will also
carry the special election set for Sept. 29."[37]   On the eve of
the election, the choice of La Follette was "taken for granted"
as "practically a certainty."[38]

Before the primary, Edward F. Dithmar, Lieutenant Governor
from 1915 to 1921, had filed as an independent candidate for
the special election as "an emergency candidate," that is, if
La Follette won the Republican nomination.[39] After the primary,
Dithmar said simply, "To my mind and to the mind of a great
many Republicans throughout Wisconsin, the emergency ex-

ists."[40] In the two days after the primary, the Stalwart leaders
held a series of discussions to determine how to defeat La Follette in the special election less than two weeks away.   Roy
P. Wilcox had planned to run as an independent, but when it
became apparent that conservative support was shifting to
Dithmar, and when Stalwart leaders put pressure on him, Wilcox withdrew.   Daniel Woodward surveyed the situation and
commented: "Mr. Dithmar, as I understand it, is a candidate
who believes in the American public school system; in the en-
forcement of laws; the separation of church and state and many
other things contained in my platform."[41]   Dithmar seemed
quite safe and received Woodward's blessing. This left Dithmar as the only anti-La Follette Republican in the race, and
he subsequently received the official endorsement of the Stalwart Republican organization.   Dithmar campaigned as a Coolidge Republican and he struck the same notes which Wilcox
has sounded during the primary: "In plain terms the question
the voters must settle is whether they want a U.S. senator who
will help, honestly and untiringly, in the progress of our nation, in harmony with President Coolidge and his declared
policies or a senator opposed to the president and his policies."[42]

The Stalwart leaders must have realized the futility of it
all.   La Follette's victory in the special election was everywhere taken for granted.   Out of a 352,135 vote total, La Follette received 237,719 votes, sixty-eight per cent of the total.
Dithmar ran second with 91,318 votes, the Socialist John Work
finished third with 11,130 votes, and Independent Democrat
William George Bruce polled 10,743 votes. La Follette carried
every county but one, the traditionally anti-La Follette Rock
County.[43]   "La Follettism swept Wisconsin off the Republican
map today," *The New York Times* said.[44]   Upon his victory
Young Bob said:

> Wisconsin, the birthplace of the Republican party,
> has rededicated itself to the Republicanism of Lin-
> coln and La Follette.   The sweeping victory won in
> the special election gives the answer of the people
> of this State to the nation that they stand solidly be-
> hind the movement founded by Robert M. La Follette

during his forty years of public service to bring Government back to the people.

In this campaign, "the issue between the forces of reaction and progress was clear-cut and simple."[45] Obviously progress had prevailed.

The Progressives claimed that Young Bob won not because he was a La Follette but because he was a Progressive. "The people of this state," *The Capital Times* said editorially, "in overwhelming measure placed their approval on Robert M. La Follette, Jr. because he was the only candidate facing the people who was pledged to carry on the policies and fight for the principles for which his father dedicated his life."[46] Progressives contended that righteousness had triumphed over political reaction. It seems clear, however, that La Follette won, not because he was a Progressive, but because he was a La Follette. "Considering the vast demonstrations connected with the La Follette funeral and the emotionalism which filled the brief campaign," Clarence Cason wrote two years later, "it would have been actually indecent for Wisconsin to fail to elect the son of Senator La Follette."[47] *The New York Times* viewed the results of the election with apprehension, calling it simply "a family affair."[48] Over twenty-five years Wisconsin had developed the habit of voting for La Follette. This was too well entrenched a habit to be easily broken. The 1925 victory was another triumph for Robert M. La Follette, Sr.

When Young Bob La Follette entered the Senate in December, there was considerable doubt that he would be recognized as a Republican. As we have seen, his father, along with Senators Brookhart, Ladd, and Frazier, had been expelled from the Republican party in the spring of 1925 because of their support of the La Follette Presidential candidacy in 1924. Young Bob was no less guilty of these sins. Immediately after the special election, Republican Senator James E. Watson of Indiana proclaimed: "We will never admit La Follette into the Republican conference in the Senate."[49] The Senate, however, was short of Republicans. The Republicans needed every vote they could muster, even a Bob La Follette, Jr. They tendered him choice committee assignments; he strongly asserted his independence from party pressure, and on these terms he accepted the assign-

ments. Frank R. Kent entitled his feature article on this incident "Little Bob Wins."[50]

Robert M. La Follette, Sr. had served as United States
Senator and as the actual political leader of the Wisconsin
Progressives. His eldest son would never play both roles. He
would serve as a Senator, one who would become increasingly
effective and influential, one who would rise to national prom-
inence in his own right in the 1930's, and one who would become a kind of Senator quite unlike his father. Yet, Young Bob
never served as a state political leader. During his first four
or five years in the Senate he paid greater attention to Wisconsin politics than he did after 1930. His name alone remained a formidable political asset for two decades, an asset
upon which he relied heavily. Probably few people in 1925
could believe that Young Bob would actually serve in the Senate longer than his father. He was, after all, merely his father's son; he was not a force to be reckoned with in his own
right. Because of this, in 1925 few people considered the
prospect of Young Bob's political career.

In his first three years in the Senate, La Follette did little
to dispel this feeling. He took the same position on issues
that his father had taken, and he voted just as his father had
voted. He also denounced the presence of United States Marines in Nicaragua, and he sponsored a resolution against a
third term for a President. In 1928 his short term expired. He
opened his campaign for re-election with a ringing reassertion
of his father's principles:

> The issues of the 1928 campaign are merely chang-
> es rung by time on the age-old question of popular
> government. Shall the United States be ruled in the
> interest of all, or in the interest of the privileged
> few? Shall the greatest experiment in popular gov-
> ernment in the world's history be directed by its men
> and women for the common good, or shall it be dic-
> tated by organized wealth determined to subvert gov-
> ernment to its own selfish ends?[51]

In June, 1928, at the Republican convention, Young Bob's pres-
entation of the Progressive platform made him something of a
national celebrity. The delegates greeted him warmly, then

voted against his program. "Hoover got the votes," a *New York Telegram* reporter wrote, but "La Follette got the cheers."[52] After the Kansas City convention, La Follette explained his rejection of the Republican platform:

> It would be sheer hypocrisy for me to announce my candidacy for the Senate on the Republican platform adopted at Kansas City. It approves the Mellon tax plan in the interest of the rich and the use of armed forces in Nicaragua without the consent of Congress, in violation of the Constitution.
>
> It denies relief to the basic industry, agriculture, and fails to meet the issue of injunctions in labor disputes, which threatens the very existence of labor organizations. It pussyfoots on the oil scandals; it evades the issue of Muscle Shoals and ignores the ruthless corruption of all the avenues of public opinion by the giant electric power companies.[53]

The general tone of his approach, and his reliance upon his father's heritage, were little different from what they had been three years before. He seemed in absolutely no danger of losing; "of his own nomination there can be no doubt," *The New York Times* reported.[54] In the September primary and November general election he won the most overwhelming victories of his career. In the primary La Follette carried every county but one, for Rock County held out again. In the general election even that bastion of anti-La Folletteism fell as he received 635,376 of the 742,645 votes cast for United States Senator. His supporters wanted to believe that it was a matter of righteousness and progressivism prevailing over evil and political reaction. His re-election, however, was simply a personal victory. In the primary the very incarnation of evil— a big businessman—won the Republican nomination for Governor over La Follette's own candidate, Congressman James Beck. In the fall campaign La Follette refused to support the Republican nominee for Governor, Walter J. Kohler, but Kohler won anyway. In the Presidential election La Follette did not specifically support Democrat Al Smith, but he very specifically opposed Republican Herbert Hoover. Nevertheless, Hoover carried Wisconsin, 544,205 to 450,259 votes.[55] That Sen-

ator La Follette contrasted his own position so sharply with
Kohler's and Hoover's and that all three triumphed indicated
that principles mattered far less and personalities far more
than many Progressives wanted to believe.

Over the course of years Robert M. La Follette, Jr. established himself as a different kind of Senator from what his
father had been. Old Bob La Follette never doubted the righteousness of his own cause. He was sustained by the un-
swerving conviction that every bit of his progressivism was
absolutely right. Young Bob had his doubts. The substance
of his speeches did not differ from his father's; they were
filled with the same ringing cries against reaction, the same
denunciations of the money power and the entrenched interests.
Like his father, Young Bob fought against all that offended his
moral sensitivities, his sense of justice. Many who knew him
well insist that throughout his career La Follette remained devoted to his father and always tried to measure his actions by
what he believed his father would have done. But he proved
to be far more conciliatory, far more willing and able to see
the other side, far readier to compromise. He had a less dynamic, less demanding personality; he was far more quiet, far
more reticent, far more judicious than his father. His father
had been an innovator, a crusading reformer, an energetic
fighter for new departures in American political life. Young
Bob was neither a crusader nor an innovator. Rather, he mas-
tered the techniques of Senatorial procedure, of legislative
craftsmanship; he understood the folkways of the Senate. He
became a "civil service Senator," a "Senator's Senator." Old
Bob had championed the direct primary and the regulation of
the railroads, issues capable of arousing widespread popular
enthusiasm. Young Bob probably considered as his major Senatorial achievement the Legislative Reorganization Act of 1946.
For all its importance, the reorganization of Congress could
hardly be expected to stir the masses. Perhaps the most striking contrast of all between father and son, the elder La Follette saw most issues and most men in terms of black and
white, the right way and the wrong way, the good guys and the
bad guys. The younger La Follette often spoke in much the
same black-and-white terms, but he developed a great will-
ingness and ability to compromise, to see the other side, to

find some good in almost everybody. He simply did not have his father's great capacity for personal animosities. "The elder La Follette was a prosecutor, a man to whom black had no shadings," Henry Pringle wrote. "Bob, in contrast, seems far more reasonable. There is not the same rigidity to his jaw. . . . One gathers that he has an ability to see the other side which his father lacked."[56] In short, Young Bob came to understand, better than his father ever did, that compromise and the good will of his colleagues were the lubricants of the legislative machinery.

In 1930 *The New York Times* said editorially, "In the Senate Bob had made a good record and has impressed his elder colleagues with his steadfastness, courage, and skill."[57] In the politically explosive summer of 1932 Mauritz Hallgren wrote:

> The most logical leader of any honestly radical movement is Robert M. La Follette. . . . He has the older man's sincerity and directness; he has proved himself as able a political strategist; but he also has something his father lacked, and that is a fundamentally sound sense of economics. It is this attribute, above all others, that has made of the younger La Follette one of the few really important and influential members of the Senate to-day. And it is this sense of economics, *plus* political skill, that the radical movement must have.[58]

In the same year Elmer Davis noted that La Follette was "the only Northwestern Progressive with a national point of view; the Senate could not afford to lose him."[59] By the early 1930's, then, Senator Robert M. La Follette, Jr. had acquired a reputation on his own, and a reputation marking him as a less controversial public figure than his father had been.

In his first fifteen years in the Senate, Young Bob La Follette became particularly associated with three major national issues: 1) unemployment relief and public works, 2) tax reform, and 3) the Civil Liberties Committee. In 1928, a year and a half before the Stock Market crash, La Follette introduced a resolution in the Senate calling for the establishment of a joint Congressional committee to study the problem of unemployment. In the months after the Crash, La Follette advocated large-scale public works as a way to put men back to work, and in 1931, along with Senator Edward P. Costigan of Colorado, he sponsored just such a program of $5,500,000,000.   Young Bob was pleased with the increased efforts in the direction of unemployment relief and public works after Franklin D. Roosevelt became President. Yet La Follette wished that the federal government would go even further.   In the spring of 1935 the Roosevelt administration proposed a new program of public works to cost $4,880,000,000; La Follette wanted twice as much. In 1937—38 Senator La Follette was frequently critical of President Roosevelt for reductions that the administration had made in public works spending.

The elder La Follette had championed the income tax long before it was adopted in 1913.   Thereafter, the La Follettes favored a graduated income tax, "taxation based on the ability to pay." During the 1930's Congress graduated the income tax sharply.   Young Bob La Follette played a prominent role in drafting this legislation, and he became recognized as one of the leading experts on taxation in the Congress.   The cry for taxation based on the ability to pay had become so ingrained in the Progressives' creed that it was difficult for them to get it out of their system. In 1946, when he was campaigning for re-election, La Follette continued to champion "taxation based on the ability to pay," even though this was a fully accepted part of the tax structure.

Possibly La Follette's most important activity in his first fifteen years in the Senate was his work as chairman of a Senate sub-committee "to make an investigation of violations of the rights of free speech and assembly and undue interference with the right of labor to organize and bargain collectively."[60] This committee was commonly known as the La Follette Civil Liberties Committee.   Organized labor looked upon this committee as an ally, especially when it conducted an investigation into the massive steel strike of 1937.   The *Literary Digest* appraised the committee's work and La Follette's role in it:

Washington correspondents noted last week that
for dignity and fairness the Civil Liberties inquiry

is on a par with the late Thomas J. Walsh's Teapot
Dome investigation of 1922—'23. This is the measure of Young Bob La Follette, who walked on the political stage twelve years ago in a pair of shoes at
least five sizes too large for him.

By general consent, he has grown into his father's
shoes—or has proved that they always were a good
fit.[61]

Senator La Follette's work on the Civil Liberties Committee
greatly enhanced his standing with organized labor.

The Great Depression gave the Progressives throughout
the nation renewed hope. For years they had been saying that
many things were wrong, but few people believed them. With
the deepening economic and social crisis the Progressives became stronger, for quite obviously many things were quite
wrong. To many Progressives it was not enough of a change
to replace the Republicans with the Democrats. They wanted
an altogether new political apparatus, a new political party
through which progressive-minded citizens could work collectively to solve the economic problems which plagued the nation. The attempt in 1924 had failed. It had failed because
popular support did not arise to demand a new political party,
because there was too much satisfaction with things as they
were. In the early 1930's, however, many Progressives believed that the economic crisis, by its very severity, had broken
enough traditional patterns of action and had generated enough
dissatisfaction with things as they were that there would be
sufficient popular support for a new political party. After the
Democrats captured national power and failed to end the economic crisis, the agitation for a third party increased in intensity. The Progressives of the Middle West came to the forefront
of this movement. Minnesota already had the Farmer-Labor
party, which was ready to join Progressives in other states to
form a new national party.

Any action for a new party in Wisconsin would be of primary concern to Senator Robert M. La Follette, Jr. Though he
gave no encouragement to the movement, he was Wisconsin's
senior Senator and the state's most prominent political per-

sonality, and he bore the magic name long associated with Progressivism. No movement in Wisconsin to form a Progressive party could possibly ignore him.

Chapter II

THE BIRTH OF THE PROGRESSIVE PARTY

Robert M. La Follette, Jr. succeeded his father in the United States Senate. He did not succeed his father as the leader of the Wisconsin Progressives, and it was not clear for several years who would fill that role. In 1926 the Progressive John J. Blaine went on to the Senate. In 1926 and 1928, however, Progressive candidates for Governor were defeated. Progressive defeats in these gubernatorial contests, coupled with Senator La Follette's overwhelming victory in 1928, indicated that the movement rested more on the popularity of La Follette than on the popularity of Progressive principles or the strength of the Progressive organization. "The iron discipline of the elder La Follette is missing," one observer noted. "Neither 'Young Bob' nor Blaine can play the game as the old Senator did."[1]

Over the years, however, Robert M. La Follette's younger son, Philip Fox La Follette, was gradually taking the reigns of Progressive leadership in his own hands. Phil was the son who was to follow in his father's footsteps. Politics flowed in his veins. He was more energetic, more politically ambitious than his older brother. In 1930 thirty-three year old Phil entered the race for Governor against the Stalwart incumbent, Walter J. Kohler. La Follette's candidacy appeared to be a sign of the Progressives' weakness; they simply had to rely on young Phil as their only chance for victory. "The fact that Phil La Follette looms as the Progressives' choice against him [Governor Kohler] is a confession that they do not believe they

25

could defeat him with any other candidate," one observer wrote.[2] This campaign submitted the popularity of the La Follette name to its greatest test, but Phil soundly defeated Governor Kohler and maintained the family habit of winning elections in Wisconsin. It was a remarkable political brother act; now that Young Bob, at thirty-five, was the senior Senator from Wisconsin, and Phil, at thirty-three, was the Governor of the state there came to be considerable interest and curiosity in these amazing La Follettes, and they received a wealth of national publicity—one article in a popular national magazine called them the "Ruling Dynasty of Wisfollette."[3] Immediately after the September, 1930, primary, one reporter wrote: "At their age there has been nothing quite like the hold the La Follette brothers have in Wisconsin. It is far stronger than the political grasp of Robert M. La Follette the elder."[4] It appeared beyond question that the young La Follettes would be a formidable political force within Wisconsin and within the nation for many years to come.

The two political roles played by the father were now divided between the two sons, a division of labor satisfactory for both brothers. Young Bob fully enjoyed his duties as a Senator, as a legislative craftsman. Yet he enjoyed neither the task of party leadership nor the rough and tumble of political campaigns; indeed, campaigning was even an unpleasant chore for him, though few who heard him on the hustings ever realized it. In striking contrast, his brother enjoyed these activities and faced most political campaigns with enthusiasm. After 1930, with his brother providing the leadership for the Wisconsin Progressives, Senator La Follette participated less frequently in state political activities.

The economic crisis undoubtedly contributed to Phil La Follette's victory in 1930. By early 1932 the Depression had become far more acute; the winds of political change were blowing fiercely across the nation and uprooting normal political patterns. Even the traditional Republicanism of Wisconsin was about to fall under this storm. The first important signal, and a dramatic one, came in the Wisconsin Presidential primary of April, 1932. In every Presidential election year after 1904 the Progressives had won control of the delegation to the Republican National Convention. In 1932 the Stalwarts reversed this trend, electing sixteen of the twenty-seven delegates. The battle between the Smith and Roosevelt forces had drawn voters into the Democratic primary, voters who probably would have supported the Progressives in the Republican primary.

Damaging as this was, an even more staggering blow to the Progressives came with the September primary. In every election since 1900 a La Follette had never been defeated. Yet, in the September, 1932, primary former Governor Kohler overwhelmed Governor Philip La Follette, 414,575 to 319,884 votes.[5] John Chapple unseated Senator John J. Blaine. The Stalwart rout of the Progressives was virtually complete, and it was impressive. The political brother act was in partial eclipse; Senator La Follette could well be concerned lest the tide which claimed his brother might sweep him out of the United States Senate in 1934.

After the primary the Progressives, to no one's surprise, found so little virtue in the Stalwarts that they could not support them. In 1928 Senator La Follette had opposed Herbert Hoover, but he had not gone all the way to outright support of Al Smith or any other Democrat. In 1932 Senator La Follette and the Wisconsin Progressives openly supported Franklin D. Roosevelt for President and Democrats Albert G. Schmedeman for Governor and F. Ryan Duffy for United States Senator. The political reverberations of 1932 shook traditionally Republican Wisconsin, and observers anticipated a Democratic victory. For once the general election in Wisconsin would be a real battle. Even before the primary, Elmer Davis wrote that "it looks as if the Democrats would carry the State this fall."[6] The predicted Democratic victory came. Roosevelt carried the state with a margin of 707,410 to 347,741 votes over Hoover, and Schmedeman defeated Kohler, 590,114 to 470,805 votes.[7] For the first time in forty years Wisconsin had a Democratic administration. Even though the candidates which they had endorsed were elected, the Progressives could see little hope in their own future. They found themselves in the unhappy position of being the minority faction within the minority party.

The upsurge in the Democratic vote had come mainly from voters who had previously supported the Progressives in the Republican primary. In the future, with their own primary vote

reduced, the Progressives would find it difficult, if not impossible, to win the Republican nominations. Even if they did win
in the primary it would be only after a protracted battle, and
then they would have to face another strenuous campaign in
the general election against the rejuvenated Democrats. It
became a simple matter of political survival for the Progressives to reconsider their status as a faction within the Republican party.

President Roosevelt and the Democrats were not all that
the Progressives wanted, but they were infinitely better than
Herbert Hoover and the Republicans. The Democrats appeared
a trifle less reactionary than the other party, and they stood
in the better position to be the permanent political instrument
of liberal action. The President seemed to be taking definite
steps to solve the Depression, and using the power of the federal government with far less restraint than Hoover had done.
Big business and monopoly capital might soon find Roosevelt
hostile to their desires for special privilege. Ralph M. Immell,
the Adjutant General of Wisconsin, and a few other La Follette
supporters, developed this argument, and urged the Progressive
faction to shift to the Democratic party.[8] Then they could better support President Roosevelt, and they could win elections.
Virtually all Wisconsin Progressives, however, opposed this
suggestion. So, too, did the Wisconsin Democrats. Before
1932 the Wisconsin Democratic party, with no expectations
of statewide victory, hoped only that the election of a Democratic President would provide them with a few tid-bits of federal patronage. Though the Democrats had never expected
power in Wisconsin, now that they had it they did not want to
lose it. They did not want to see their recently acquired positions fall into the hands of an invading army of Progressives.
For their own part, the Progressives did not seriously consider
taking over the Democratic party. They believed that the Wisconsin Democrats were just as hopelessly reactionary as the
Stalwart Republicans. "The Democratic Party in Wisconsin
was merely a political shell manned by job conscious people,"
Progressive Tom Amlie later recalled. "It was inevitable that
when the Democratic Party won out in the State in 1932, that
it was a group of conservative politicans [*sic*] who came to
power. The conservative character of the Democrat party did

not change in the 1930's."[9] Furthermore, the Democratic party probably would not long remain in power in Wisconsin; its success was simply a temporary phenomenon.

For most Wisconsin Progressives remaining in the Republican party was impractical, and joining the Democrats was unthinkable. The only other alternative was to form an entirely new party. In early 1933 former Progressive Congressman Thomas R. Amlie discussed this possibility with Phil La Follette:

> In April of 1933, I had several discussions with Phil La Follette in Washington, regarding the future course of the Progressives in Wisconsin. We were agreed that the Progressives could not hope to liberalize the Republican Party and that if this was true, we did not belong in the Republican Party. The possibility of going into the Democrat Party was mentioned by myself, but this suggestion was emphatically rejected by Phil La F. He pointed out that the Democrat members of the Wis. legislature were just as reactionary as the Republicans and that it would not be politically feasible to go where we would not be welcome. He was sympathetic to the idea of a separate Progressive Party but only if there was an overwhelming demand by the rank and file for such a course.[10]

In September, 1933, the United Conference for Progressive Political Action, meeting in Chicago, created the Farmer-Labor Political Federation and selected Tom Amlie as its chairman. The Federation sought to form a national Progressive party, but it realized that the practical beginnings could only be made on a state-by-state basis.

In late 1933 and early 1934 many conferences of labor, farm organization and political leaders discussed the future of the Wisconsin Progressives. "For a number of months, the Milwaukee Sentinel referred to the movement as Mr. Amlie's Third Party," Tom Amlie has recalled with a noticeable feeling of pride.[11] The strongest sentiment among the Progressives was a desire to form their own party. "Progressives in many parts of the state, particularly in agricultural and dairying

areas, are outspoken in behalf of a third party," one reporter
wrote in February, 1934.[12]   The Farmers' Holiday Association
and the Wisconsin Cooperative Milk Pool joined the movement.
Two state labor leaders, Joseph Padway, counsel for the Wisconsin Federation of Labor, and Henry Ohl, Jr., President of the
Wisconsin Federation of Labor, had favored a new party as
early as July, 1931, but at that time, the La Follettes were "too
much interested in getting themselves elected on the Republican ticket" to go in for the idea.[13]   In late 1933 the La Follettes seemed much less likely to get elected on the Republican ticket, and Padway and Ohl became optimistic that their
hopes would materialize.

The Wisconsin Progressives charged that the two old reactionary parties made the formation of a third party essential,
but it was political necessity, more than anything else, which
forced them to consider this move; they did not see how they
could win *except* as a separate party.   In the early months of
1934, Phil La Follette saw this sentiment gaining momentum
among the Progressives, and he started to play an active role
directing the movement.   He realized, however, that only his
brother could speak for the Progressives with the authority of
leadership in whatever they decided to do.   "Privately, Phil
La F. was very much interested in the success of the venture,"
Tom Amlie has recalled, "but publicly he took the position that
Bob La F. was the spokesman for the Progressives."[14] Because
Robert M. La Follette, Jr. was the major Progressive office-
holder, and because he bore the magic name of La Follette, the
Wisconsin Progressives would need his support if they wanted
to leave the Republican party.

Senator La Follette opposed any action to take the Progressives out of the Republican party, but, characteristically,
he was in no mood to impose his will upon anyone else.   He
approached the problem with the attitude: "I don't want to
leave the Republican party. I am opposed to joining the Democrats, or to the formation of a new party. That is my opinion.
Nevertheless, if the Progressives of Wisconsin, the rank-and-
file, decide to form a third party, I shall lend them my support."
President Roosevelt and Democratic National Chairman James
A. Farley wanted La Follette in the Democratic party.[15] For one
thing, Senator La Follette had supported most of the Roosevelt

program in Congress. Furthermore, he could add some permanence to the present popularity of Democrats in Wisconsin. Finally, to get Senator La Follette into the Democratic party might prevent him from participating in any third party activity which could undermine Roosevelt's strength on the left. Senator La Follette quickly rejected any idea of joining the Democrats. He claimed that the Democrats in Wisconsin were hopelessly reactionary, that the Schmedeman administration was out of step with the New Deal, that on the issues which came before the state Legislature the Democrats usually joined with the Stalwart Republicans. Moreover, he knew that his brother emphatically opposed joining the Democrats. As usual, Young Bob did not want to do anything politically disagreeable to his younger brother.

But the Wisconsin Progressives had rejected the notion of moving to the Democratic party almost the moment it arose. The real question was whether the Progressives would remain in the Republican party or withdraw from it and form their own party. Robert M. La Follette, Jr. opposed the formation of a separate Progressive party. From his own vantage point, he feared that leaving the Republican party would complicate his position in the Senate and affect his committee positions. In addition, he feared that such a drastic political venture might endanger his chances for re-election in 1934. "Seeking re-election on a new party ticket against candidates of the well organized major parties," Mark Byers wrote, "requires for success that he wean from long-established party habits scores of thousands of voters."[16] Finally, his own restrained temperament caused him to hesitate before taking any political action which was new and dramatically different. Robert M. La Follette, Jr. was a cautious and conservative man, judicious in his approach to all problems. He was far less impulsive than his brother, or his father for that matter, and he would never take a step without carefully surveying the prospects. "I was the engineer," Phil La Follette has said, "he was the brake."[17]

Young Bob had long served as a brake. Some close associates believe that he urged his father against a third party Presidential bid in 1924.[18] In March, 1931, five Progressive Senators, Republicans La Follette, George Norris and Bronson

Cutting, and Democrats Burton K. Wheeler and Edward P. Costigan called a conference to formulate a program for the economic crisis. The conference disavowed any desire to form a new party. For his own part Senator La Follette said: "In my judgment new parties are created only when there is, a sufficient upswelling of public sentiment on important public questions. At this time, or in the near future, I can foresee no third-party movement of sufficient strength to become a factor in the next Presidential campaign."[19] In 1933, as the movement towards a separate party for Wisconsin Progressives gathered mementum, Senator La Follette expressed his doubts to his brother. "I sense your desire for action," Young Bob wrote, "and yet all my training leads me to want to know where we are going before we leap."[20] In February, 1934, Bob wrote that he had weighed all of his brother's arguments, yet he was still "in doubt on the practical aspects of the situation."[21] He looked at his own position in the Senate and his contest for re-election, he contemplated the practicality of a third party, and he quivered in doubt. Senator La Follette was not ready to jump, but he was allowing himself to be pushed into the breach.

In February, 1934, Secretary of State Theodore Dammann, Herman L. Ekern, and Senator La Follette sent a letter to Progressive leaders, which said simply: "It seems the unanimous desire of all Progressives that a conference be held in the near future for consideration and discussion of matters of importance."[22] The leadership conference met on March 3, 1934, in Madison, and attracted more than four hundred delegates. Norman Clapp has heard from other Progressives that on the evening before the meeting Senator La Follette had some old friends at the family farm at Maple Bluff. He told them that he personally opposed the idea of a separate party for it would complicate his position as a Senator. Yet, La Follette continued, he would go along with the new party if it were in the best interests of the Progressive movement, if there were overwhelming support for it. In later years La Follette told many Progressives privately that originally he had opposed the formation of the party.[23]

La Follette spoke to the meeting and expressed his views on the matters which were of the greatest concern to him, the

Depression and President Roosevelt's attempt to solve it. He said that he had judged Roosevelt's policies by one standard: "Whenever I felt that his policies were going in the direction of restoring the purchasing power of the people, I have supported them. Those which it seemed to me were deflationary in character I have opposed." Then La Follette discussed in vague terms the future of the Wisconsin Progressives:

> It is not important, so far as I have observed, whether a man calls himself a Republican, a Democrat, or a Progressive. The public record teaches the voter how to test the fidelity of his representative. . . .
>
> We have before us one of the most momentous decisions Progressives in this state have ever been called upon to make. I appeal to you not to consider your decision on the basis of the political fortunes of any individual, but on the basis of the welfare of the Progressive movement and the people of Wisconsin. I want you to know that I would not hesitate to throw what political future I may have in this state and the nation into the hopper with your decision.[24]

Senator La Follette was not the fighting leader urging his followers to hoist aloft the banner of a new party. He was not prepared to lead the Progressives in the formation of a separate party, nor was he prepared to lead the minority which opposed the new venture. He was saying that he would allow the Progressives to point out the trail down which he would lead them. As Mark Byers put it: "The Senator's followers demand that he lead them into the breach. Not to do so would probably be the ruin of his great personal following—political death even surer than the consequences of a stout if unsuccessful campaign at the head of a new party."[25]

The majority sentiment at the conference undoubtedly favored a separate party, but there was an undercurrent of doubt and hesitation. Before the Progressives could make a final decision they had to face the legal obstacle of placing a new party on the ballot. A number of their leaders, including Herman Ekern, Thomas R. Amlie, Philip La Follette and William T. Evjue, brought "an original action" in the Wisconsin Supreme

Court "to secure a declaratory judgment construing and inter-
preting those provisions of Chapter Five of the Wisconsin
Statutes for 1933 relating to the formation of a new political
party."[26]   The Supreme Court decided that the law would not
prevent the inclusion of a new party on the ballot in 1934, if
it could secure approximately 10,000 signatures.   The legal
road lay clear; now the Progressives merely had to call a convention to go through the formalities of launching their new
party.

The convention met in Fond du Lac on May 19.   Senator
La Follette had not taken any active part in the preparations
for the convention, leaving this in the hands of his brother.
There was little doubt what action this gathering would take.
By a vote of 252 to forty-four, the La Follette Progressives
established their own party. The story has been told that William T. Evjue, chairman of the convention, called for a unanimous vote.   "The forty-four dissenters refused to stand. . . .
Chairman Evjue ordered the pianist to play the national anthem.
The forty-four dissenters stood up and the vote was unanimous."[27]   Then, by a vote of 236 to forty-one, the convention
rejected "Farmer-Labor" as their party label, and adopted the
designation "Progressive."

After the convention had launched the Progressive party,
Senator La Follette spoke to the delegates. First he analyzed
the weaknesses in the American economy and President Roosevelt's attempts to remedy them.   "It is obvious that we can
produce all the wealth necessary to insure the comfort of the
American people. We have failed, however, to solve the problem of distribution. Until a political party attacks that problem
with courage and wisdom we cannot hope to attain genuine re-
covery or a stable future."   Even though at times President
Roosevelt has strayed from the path of progressivism, he de-
serves our support; he has faced his task with courage.   Yet,
we cannot enter the Democratic party for it is hopelessly reactionary, and the reactionaries within the party masquerade
"as supporters of President Roosevelt."   What course should
we follow?   The present party structure is unsatisfactory; we
need a party realignment in the United States. "It is my clear
conviction that equal opportunity cannot become a reality and
security in the enjoyment of our abundant resources cannot be

attained, without a party free from the control of organized wealth and frankly dedicated to the interests and aspirations of the mass of the people." Yet, we must give very serious consideration before we decide that now is the time to embark upon the formation of this new party. "Many people believe my personal political welfare would be served in the coming election by the organization of a new party. I refuse to be guided in this momentous decision by its effect on the political fortune of any candidate or individual. I am not interested in a political manoeuver that merely promotes my own or any one else's candidacy. I shall only be interested in a permanent organization which may spring from the wish of the people for a more effective instrument to advance the progressive principles of Thomas Jefferson, Abraham Lincoln, and Robert M. La Follette." We cannot base this decision on its effects on the fortunes of Bob La Follette, or Phil La Follette, or anyone else. If, however, we do sail forth in our new party, we shall encounter some formidable obstacles. "I do not under-estimate the resources that will be arrayed against us in this campaign. The daily press and the corporate wealth of the state will be massed behind our opponents. I know what that campaign will cost in the co-operative efforts of all who love progressive principles and are willing to fight for them." Despite these formidable obstacles, if the Progressives of Wisconsin want to form their own party, then let us do so:

> No group of leaders or delegates, however great their enthusiasm, can create an enduring party. It is within their power, however, to afford the people the opportunity to create a party.
>
> I am in complete accord with the action this conference has taken to that end. I believe the necessity for a new third party exists. If the time has arrived for its formation, then the people of this state in their response to the action of this conference and to the petitions required by law for place on the ballot will create a party and will control it so long as it deserves to live.[28]

Senator La Follette's speech, after the convention had launched the third party, still expressed a note of hesitancy and doubt.

Nevertheless, he cast his lot with the new Progressive party
of Wisconsin.

At once, the problem of candidates confronted the new-
born party. Senator La Follette would head the ticket as a
candidate for re-election; the most perplexing question was
who would run for Governor. The logical candidate would be
his younger brother, but that would put two La Follettes on the
ballot at the same time. In the days immediately following the
Fond du Lac Convention, Senator La Follette held a series of
meetings at the family farm in Maple Bluff in an attempt to find
a candidate other than Phil to run for Governor.[29]   He wanted
to avoid overwhelming Wisconsin with La Follettes. Yet, Bob
had left the leadership of the Progressives to his brother, so
that now they did not see any other alternative, any other possible candidate.   "Some potentially winning substitute for
Philip La Follette has been sought," one reporter wrote. "The
search has proved unavailing. The Progressive party has come
to the conclusion that it cannot get along with both La Follettes."[30]   Phil La Follette entered the race for Governor. The
political brother act would meet its stiffest challenge.

The Wisconsin Progressives ran on a platform national in
scope.   "Our economic system has failed," the platform said
simply. In order to solve the economic crisis, "we must have
a political realignment that will place the exploiting reactionary on the one side and the producer, consumer, independent business and professional interests on the other. . . . Ac-
cordingly, Progressives in Wisconsin, cutting loose from all
connections with the two old reactionary parties in this crisis,
have founded a new national party under the name Progressive
party."[31] The platform, which covered mainly national issues,
was not as radical as Tom Amlie had wanted, but it was radical enough that a writer in *The New Republic* could refer to
the "Left Turn in Wisconsin"; they took the left turn, Wallace
Sayre concluded, because they "have fortunately recognized
that winning Wisconsin has become a matter of capturing its
cities, and they are aware that the new economic and social
profile of the state demands urbanization in both platform and
personnel."[32]

Upon opening his own campaign, Senator La Follette explained why he had supported President Roosevelt but had not

joined the Democratic party.   "This reactionary group, which controlled the party prior to his nomination, has yielded only temporarily to his fine personality and the sheer power of his office.   The reactionary Democrats have not surrendered and only await a favorable opportunity once more to assert their control."[33]   La Follette's own four-point platform reflected a position to the left of Roosevelt, especially the last two points:

1. The farmer is entitled to a profit on his invest-
ment above the cost of production.
2. Labor must have the right to organize without interference from employers.   There must be shorter hours, a shorter week, and wages which will give a comfortable life.
3. The people should control credit through a gov-
ernment-owned central bank, which will make cen-
tralization of credit in private hands impossible.
4. If the private employment fails, then the gov-
ernment should provide every person able and willing to work with a job at decent wages.[34]

As usual, outside support converged on Wisconsin to aid Senator La Follette.   Mayor Fiorello La Guardia of New York City, Republican Senator Gerald P. Nye of North Dakota, and Democratic Senators Edward P. Costigan of Colorado and Robert F. Wagner of New York all came to Wisconsin to speak for the Senator. "Carpet-baggers," cried John B. Chapple, the Re-
publican nominee for the Senate.   The Democratic Senatorial nominee, John M. Callahan, said: "I believe that the people want to hear what the candidates have to say themselves, not the nice things gentlemen from Montana, New York, or Texas may say about them."[35]

Senator La Follette generally had supported President Roosevelt's program in Congress, and he praised the President in the summer of 1934. The Progressives wondered how Roosevelt would respond to all the nice things La Follette had said about him. In early June Bob wrote to his brother that Senator George Norris had talked with the President, and that Roosevelt "was very much interested in my re-election to the Sen-
ate and that he was having Mr. Farley take the matter up with the Democratic leaders in Wisconsin in an effort to have some-

thing done that would be helpful to my candidacy." If these
efforts failed, then at the right moment the President would
"make a statement that if he were a citizen of Wisconsin he
would be doing all in his power in this campaign to bring about
my re-election to the Senate."[36] In a press conference later in
June the President said: "My own personal hope is that they
will find some way of sending Bob La Follette back here. But
I cannot compel the Democracy of Wisconsin to go ahead and
nominate him."[37] Wisconsin Democrats were jealous that the
Roosevelt administration was courting Senator La Follette.
They believed that they could elect one of their own men, and
they wanted the President's help.

In early August President Roosevelt passed through Wisconsin, and at Green Bay both Wisconsin Senators, Young Bob
La Follette and Democrat F. Ryan Duffy, shared the platform
with the President. Roosevelt said, much to the chagrin of the
state Democrats, "Your two Senators, Bob La Follette and Ryan
Duffy, both old friends of mine, and many others, have worked
with me in maintaining excellent co-operation between the
executive and legislative branches of the government. I take
this opportunity of expressing my gratitude to them." The
President also paid tribute to Democratic Governor Albert G.
Schmedeman.[38] This was as much as Roosevelt said about La
Follette during the campaign, but Progressives considered his
remarks an endorsement of the Senator. After the President's
statement Wisconsin Democrats, in their literature and in their
speeches, were relatively silent on the Senatorial race.

In the September primary the Progressives ran behind the
Democrats and barely ahead of the Republicans. "The La Fol-
lettian third party doesn't look like a healthy child," *The New
York Times* commented.[39] Yet the Progressive party had no
primary contests to attract voters. In the weeks before the
election Young Bob La Follette was such a heavy favorite to
win re-election that the race for Senator generated little excitement. His brother, in contrast, was a distinct underdog.
"Phil La Follette is not so popular [as his brother]," one reporter wrote. "His one term as Governor furnished basis for
criticism."[40] While Bob was running as the incumbent, Phil
was trying to unseat the present Governor. The November
election produced the expected victory for Senator La Follette.

He won with 440,513 votes to 223,438 votes for Democrat Callahan and 210,569 votes for Republican Chapple. He received
just under forty-eight per cent of the total vote, the first time
in his career he won with less than an absolute majority, and
he carried all but five counties—Portage, Green Lake, Rich-
land, Rock, and Walworth.   The new party showed surprising
strength when Phil La Follette unexpectedly defeated Governor
Schmedeman, 373,093 to 359,467 votes.[41] A Progressive, Theodore Dammann, was elected Secretary of State, while Democrats won the three other state offices.   Progressives won
seven of Wisconsin's ten seats in the House of Representatives, thirteen of the thirty-three State Senatorships and forty-
five of the one hundred places in the state Assembly.   The La
Follettes had led their party to a remarkably strong showing
less than six months after its birth.   It was a triumphant beginning.

   Throughout the 1920's the Progressives believed that both
major parties were wrong, that there should be a new party for
them and their cause. In 1934, they were forced to form a new
party simply to stay alive politically.   Nevertheless, the men
who started the Progressive party of Wisconsin saw their efforts as the first step in the formation of a national Progressive
party. "The Progressive party of the state of Wisconsin is not
a third party," Mayor La Guardia told a Milwaukee audience
during the 1934 campaign. "It is destined to be a new national
party."[42] Wisconsin Progressives hoped that La Guardia was
right, and they looked forward to a national existence. "There
is no reason why this can't be accomplished before 1940,"
Governor La Follette said in the summer of 1935.[43] Senator La
Follette remained less interested in a national Progressive
party than his brother. After a conference at the White House
in late 1934, La Follette told reporters that he and the President agreed on the issues of the day.   On the new party, the
Senator repeated his belief that the Depression would produce
a "political realignment," and continued:

> In my opinion the victory of the Progressive party
> in Wisconsin, within six months after it was organized
> there, is significant to this extent—it is a practical
> demonstration of what many have contended theoreti-

cally, namely, that a new party with a sound and far-
reaching program to meet the issues created by the
economic crisis would draw its support from the farmers, wage-earners, independent business and professional men and women, since, after all, the interests of those people are the same.[44]

Senator La Follette's words were less enthusiastic than most
leaders of the new party wanted to hear. They anticipated that,
eventually, the Progressives of both major parties would join
together, and the reactionaries of both old parties would be
driven together.   Then the American voter would face the de-
lightfully clear-cut choice of progress or reaction, of virtue or
vice. This would happen sooner or later. In 1935 and 1936 the
two La Follettes emphasized that it would be later.   They did
not envisage a national Progressive party for the 1936 election.

In 1935 and 1936 the Progressives of Wisconsin chose to
work in harmony with the national Democratic administration.
President Roosevelt's support for Senator La Follette in 1934
had undercut the state Democrats; furthermore, the Wisconsin
Democrats saw many choice patronage plums going to the Progressives.   Ralph M. Immell, a long-time La Follette family
friend, received appointment as director of the Wisconsin public works program. The La Follettes continued to give support
to Roosevelt's domestic policies, and they were pleased that
the administration had expanded its programs of public works
and relief. In the 1936 campaign the La Follettes and the Progressive party of Wisconsin supported President Roosevelt.
Senator La Follette served as chairman of the National Progressive Conference, which worked for the President's re-
election.   "Progressive-minded citizens must close ranks to
face the forces of reaction which are solidly behind Governor
Landon," Senator La Follette said.[45]   Roosevelt's triumph in
Wisconsin was as impressive as it was throughout the nation.
He carried the state by more than a two-to-one margin.   For
the Progressives this was to be their banner year. They swept
all five state-wide offices and gained almost a majority in the
state Legislature.   They returned their seven Representatives
to Congress. Never again would the Progressive party of Wisconsin achieve such success.

The winter of 1937—38 witnessed the nadir of Franklin D. Roosevelt's Presidency. His power and effectiveness had declined; his prestige reached its lowest point. He had lost his battle over the Supreme Court. He had produced a strong outcry with his Quarantine speech of October 5, 1937. He was faced with the terribly embarrassing recession of 1937; here the savior of the American economy, the man who had slowly but surely put the country back on its feet, confronted an economic recession he could not explain. In the early months of 1938 Roosevelt's future seemed bleak, and his retirement from the Presidency after 1940 seemed virtually certain. When Roosevelt had been in his heydey there was talk of an unprecedented third term, but even were he at the height of his popularity in 1940 his candidacy for a third term would provoke strong and violent opposition. With his power and prestige sliding to its lowest point in 1938, a third term seemed unthinkable. It appeared perfectly clear that on January 20, 1941, a man other than Franklin Delano Roosevelt would take the oath of office as President of the United States.

Perhaps, Progressives felt, the new President could be one of them. Perhaps, by 1940, the Progressives of Wisconsin could unite with other state parties throughout the land, perhaps they could become a fully grown national party, perhaps they could place their own man in the White House. This thought intrigued many Progressives, but to Governor Philip F. La Follette of Wisconsin it became almost an obsession. If there were to be a genuine movement to form a new national party, he wanted to lead it. At the third anniversary celebration of the Progressive party, on May 19, 1937, Governor La Follette said: "The Progressive party looks forward to a national existence and to a national political realignment. The time is close at hand for the formation of a new national alignment which will defeat the reactionary forces of America, just as the Progressive party has defeated the reactionary forces in Wisconsin."[46] In statements later that year, the Governor asserted that a political realignment would come by 1940. In 1937 and 1938 he laid his plans with great care, talking extensively with farm and labor leaders and Progressives throughout the nation. Secrecy enshrouded his specific plans. He kept them mainly to himself, revealing very little of them to

even his closest associates.[47] In April, 1938, Governor La Follette delivered a series of radio speeches, extolling the accomplishments of Wisconsin under his administration, charging
that the Roosevelt administration had failed to solve the problem of unemployment and blaming the President for not prevent-
ing the recession of 1937—38. He said that he and his brother
had broken with the administration in 1937 when it trimmed expenditures.   On April 28, 1938, at the Stock Pavilion of the
University of Wisconsin, Governor La Follette climaxed his
activities with a dramatic, mass meeting, at which he launched
the National Progressives of America. Neither the Republicans
nor the Democrats, the Governor said, had been able to solve
the problem of unemployment. A new Progressive party would
do just that. "Make no mistake, this is NOT a *third* party. As
certain as the sun rises, we are launching THE party of our
time."[48]   After his speech, "reporters were sure that history
had been made—perhaps even to the degree it had been at
Ripon, Wisconsin, eighty-four years before, when the Republican party was founded. The young Progressive, they said to
one another, had hit Roosevelt where it hurt."[49]   Governor La
Follette's mass meeting had attracted front-page headlines
throughout the nation.
     Since 1934 Senator Robert M. La Follette, Jr. had said
publicly that a national Progressive party was necessary. After
the 1936 election he declared: "We're undoubtedly gaining
some ground, both in this state and outside, although nothing
can be done overnight, and I've always contended that we must
build by States, that we can't start immediately on a national
scale."[50] In April, 1938, Senator La Follette publicly endorsed
his brother's activities. In Chicago a few days before the
Madison meeting, he said that only time will tell whether Phil's
actions would produce a third party. He added, "I have long
said there is a need for a political realignment."[51] The next
day in Madison, the Senator said that he and his brother were
in this together. "A national third party is inevitable and now
is the time to form one."[52] He asserted that he was "in it all
the way."[53] He did not attend the Madison meeting which
launched the National Progressives, but he sent a message
which said: "It is clear that if democracy is to survive and
our free institutions are to be preserved in this crisis, there

must be a genuine political realignment."[54] Senator La Follette had no choice other than to support his brother, for he simply could not afford to split with him. Phil supplied all the energy and all the resources, and certainly without him the National Progressives would never have sprung to life. Yet, Bob seemed as fully responsible for the venture as Phil; the press spoke of it as "the La Follettes' new party."

On May 9 Senator La Follette delivered a radio speech supporting the National Progressives of America. The United States, La Follette said, still faced huge, unsolved domestic problems. "In short we have practically solved the problem with which mankind has been wrestling since the dawn of civilization—the problem of production. Instead of utilizing these enormous facilities for producing wealth we are confronted with the greatest paradox in history—insecurity, misery, privation and want in the midst of political plenty." Both old parties are incapable of meeting the problem. "Can there be any hope for united action, essential to the solution of the complex and fundamental problems of our day, through the outworn machinery of the two old political parties? . . . The truth is that the Democratic party is split wide open. The bitter factional fight has paralyzed it. . . . It is clear that Old Guard Republicans dominate and control the party." Progressives must act in harmony to solve these problems:

> Confronted with the political situation, which I have tried to analyze tonight, Progressives have launched a movement to organize a new national political party. They have no illusions as to the size of the task but they believe we must have a thorough-going political realignment which will put an end to the factionalism in our party machinery which has proved so costly to the cause of democratic government in other nations.
>
> The new party is not a political maneuver timed for 1938 or 1940 or any succeeding election. It is too much to expect complete agreement among progressives as to the time for inaugurating a new movement. Those who have a stake in the present political machinery will never believe that any year, now or in the future, is the right time to begin.

After listing the cardinal Progressive principles, La Follette concluded with the ringing declaration: "Progressives have reaffirmed those broad general principles and declared that it is their solemn determination to forge a national political instrumentality which will safeguard these rights."[55]   Senator La Follette's speech expressed support for the National Progressives of America, but it was not a fighting battle-cry to fire Progressives throughout the nation with the enthusiasm and the determination to flock to the new banner. It was this enthusiasm and determination that the National Progressives needed so badly in May, 1938.

Senator La Follette was willing to say that a new party was necessary, but he was unwilling to do anything to bring it about.   In actual fact, he had opposed the formation of the National Progressives of America. He felt that it was "wrong, ill-advised."[56]   He expressed some of his apprehensions to his brother.   Phil was aware of Bob's lack of enthusiasm for this venture.[57] Senator La Follette had been in Washington at the time of the Stock Pavilion meeting.   The naval expansion bill, sponsored by the administration, was then before Congress and Senator La Follette opposed it.   He found this a convenient excuse to absent himself from Madison on April 28. He believed that he could not avoid voicing support for the National Progressives, but his heart was not in it. He did not want to do anything politically disagreeable to his brother, yet he was firmly associated with a venture that he did not like.   A close observer later wrote, "Bob usually goes along with Phil.   Phil has not always done so with Bob."[58]   In this case, Bob went along with Phil.   Yet he kept his displeasure to himself. Several of his friends have recalled that he evaded talk of the subject, that he never liked to discuss it.[59]

The National Progressives of America complicated Senator La Follette's position.   He had been on very good terms with President Roosevelt, and each man had great respect for the other.   It was true that in late 1937 and early 1938 Senator La Follette wished that the President would not curtail public works expenditures but increase them.   This, however, was not new for La Follette; he had always urged more public works than the President sponsored.   In general, the friendship and cordiality between the President and the Wisconsin Senator was so great that there was widespread talk of La Follette as Roosevelt's choice to succeed him. In March, 1935, a boomlet appeared for Senator La Follette as the President's running mate in 1936.[60] "If Roosevelt thought of any of the Progressives as his successor," Arthur M. Schlesinger, Jr. has written, "it was certainly the quiet, tough-minded Senator from Wisconsin."[61] Harry Hopkins' notes indicated a conversation he had with the President in the spring of 1938 in which Roosevelt talked about Senator La Follette. Hopkins' notes said "fine—later—Secretary of State soon."[62] In discussing the new party, *Time* said "as recently as last summer not a few observers got the impression that 'Young Bob' was likely to be the President's personal choice as his successor."[63] Senator La Follette may not have been Roosevelt's choice as his successor, but at least the Senator enjoyed a close political and personal relationship with the President. The National Progressives, implicitly hostile to Roosevelt, undermined this relationship. Senator La Follette tried to balance his loyalty to his brother with a desire to remain on good terms with the President. He supported his brother's venture with a radio speech; yet, in that speech, he went on to say: "The irreconciliable factional cleavage in the Democratic party has thus far impaired and now threatens to destroy the effectiveness of one of the great liberal leaders of modern time—Franklin D. Roosevelt."[64] In the final analysis, however, Senator La Follette's lot was cast with his brother. Arthur Krock, the head of the Washington bureau of *The New York Times*, wrote that summer that the President was friendly towards La Follette until the Senator "started a new national party."[65]

"A seven day wonder throughout the country," the National Progressives of America were called.[66] Phil's mass meeting received enormous publicity, but the excitement abated very shortly, and the movement seemed near death within a few days of its birth. It did not, as Governor La Follette had hoped it would, attract many liberals and progressives from around the nation to its banner. Many liberals expressed the fear that, at a time when they must unite behind the President, the new party would split their forces and insure the triumph of reaction. "It is much too early for a final judgment," a writer in *The Nation* said a few days after the Stock Pavilion meet-

ing, "but at this time and distance Phil La Follette's effort to
launch a National Progressive Party looks and sounds like a
dud. . . . It appears to be strictly a family enterprise, and one
may question to what extent Bob's heart is in it, notwithstand-
ing his public indorsement."[67] The new party was called many
things, from semi-fascistic to a venture which was "somewhat
comic."[68] Because of its cross-within-a-circle emblem, which
evoked thoughts of Hitler's swastika, its one-man dominance,
and the implication that this party would be the sole political
instrument of the future, and because many liberals and progressives feared that it would split their forces, the National
Progressives of America failed to get off the ground.

In the fall of 1938, Governor La Follette ran for an unprecedented fourth term. Victory in Wisconsin was essential to
keep alive any hopes for the national party. In that year a
coalition of Democrats and Republicans united in an attempt
to defeat the Progressives. Robert K. Henry ran for both the
Democratic and Republican gubernatorial nominations. He won
only the Democratic nomination, and then withdrew in favor of
the Republican nominee, Julius P. Heil. In the November election the Republicans, with the support of many Democrats,
overwhelmed the Progressives and moved into a position of
undisputed dominance within the state. They won absolute
control of the state Legislature. They won eight of the ten
House seats. Alexander Wiley was elected to the United States
Senate. Julius P. Heil defeated Governor La Follette, 543,675
to 353,381 votes.[69] This defeat in Wisconsin was a fatal blow
for the National Progressives of America.

By 1938 Phil La Follette had become less popular in Wisconsin than his older brother; in his six years as Governor he
had antagonized many people. Furthermore, his plans in 1938
for a national party had split the state party. "In Wisconsin
the Progressive Party was sharply divided," Tom Amlie has
recalled, "between the Progressives who followed Phil La F.
in his National Progressives of America and the Progressives
who believed with Bill Evjue that this was a fascistic under-
taking. It was plain that with this division the Progressive
Party was finished. In the meantime FDR had gone so far in
providing leadership for organized labor and liberals generally
that there was but little room for a third political party."[70]

Finally, towards the end of his six years as Governor, some former associates felt that Phil saw himself as the incarnation of the Progressive movement.[71] The Senator, on the other hand, was far more popular with Progressive leaders and with the Wisconsin voters generally. He was less aggressive, less ambitious for his own political career. More than that, he was in Washington, away from the rough and tumble of state politics, fighting for measures in Congress popular to the Progressives back home.

Between the La Follette brothers outward harmony prevailed; privately, there had been tension both in 1934 and in 1938. "They are loyal to each other" as they are to their father, Elmer Davis said in 1939, after he had spent many weeks following Governor La Follette's political activities. "If they disagree (as many people believed they disagreed on the advisability of starting the national party, at least at that time and in that way) they disagree in private and outwardly present a united front."[72] Robert La Follette purposely deferred to his brother on the conduct of state political matters. After his defeat in 1938, Phil La Follette withdrew from state affairs and effective leadership of the Wisconsin Progressives. No other Progressive stepped forward to fill the breach. Senator La Follette did not take this burden upon himself. In its first four years the Progressive party enjoyed strong leadership. After Phil La Follette withdrew the party never again had a real political leader.

In the 1930's Robert M. La Follette, Jr. had acquired a reputation on his own. Many regarded him as the likely Presidential candidate for a national Progressive party in 1940. As for a leader for a national third party, Oswald Garrison Villard wrote, "so far as the Washington of today is concerned, the finger of fate seems to many to point to Bob."[73] A *New York Times* reporter examined the 1940 Presidential race three years ahead of time, and saw Senator La Follette as the possible leader of a farmer-labor coalition.[74] His name, his conscientious devotion to his Senatorial duties, his consistent support of progressive measures, and his Civil Liberties Committee gave Robert M. La Follette, Jr. a reputation as a respectable statesman. Perhaps he might have led a national Progressive party if the problems confronting the United States continued to be domestic affairs.

In late September, 1938, barely a month before the elections, far away from the American political scene, four European leaders signed the pact of Munich.   Peace momentarily appeared at hand, but for the next eleven months Europe headed down the road to war.   In March, 1939, Germany seized the rest of Czechoslovakia. On August 23, 1939, Germany and the Soviet Union signed a non-aggression pact which opened the way to Germany's attack on Poland. In the early morning hours of September 1, 1939, the German armies streamed across the Polish border, precipitating the Second World War.   Munich, Germany's seizure of the rest of Czechoslovakia, the German-Soviet alliance, and the declaration of war in September brought foreign affairs to the front pages of the newspapers in an America which had been concerned almost exclusively with domestic problems.   A month after war had broken out, Senator La Follette delivered a radio speech, voicing apprehension at the possibility of American involvement:

> War is democracy's greatest enemy.   It cannot live under war conditions.   If we enter the war, our own democracy would be the first casualty. . . .
>
> Once we have taken sides through action by our Government in order to make arms available to England and France, the pressure will be terrific to get us into the war. . . .
>
> We either make up our minds to stay out of this war in Europe or by a series of steps we will ultimately find ourselves in it.[75]

In the remaining months of 1939 and through the first three months of 1940, no one was fighting; it was a strange war. Then, in April, 1940, the German blitzkrieg struck and took Denmark and Norway. In May and June the Low Countries and France swiftly fell to the might of the German armies.   Great Britain trembled before the threat of an invasion. The sword of Damocles hung over America.   Senator La Follette feared that foreign affairs would divert attention from America's pressing and unsolved domestic problems.   He did not want the American people to become involved in the war in Europe.

The European war generated controversy in America which

cut across existing political lines. President Roosevelt was in the last year of his second term. In the summer of 1940 the war in Europe and a Presidential election confronted the American people. In Wisconsin, the Progressive party was without effective leadership and without power. It limped into the starting gate for the 1940 campaign. Senator Robert M. La Follette, Jr. was the major Progressive office-holder, and he faced re-election. Upon his success depended the future of the Progressive party.

Chapter III

THE ELECTION OF 1940

Nineteen-forty produced one of the most exciting and one of
the most bitter Presidential elections in American history. In
June, at the Republican Convention in Philadelphia the gal-
leries shouted "We want Willkie," and to the surprise of just
about everyone, they got him. In July, at the Democratic Convention in Chicago delegates shouted "We want Roosevelt,"
and to the surprise of no one, they got him. Never before had
a President of the United States placed himself before the
American people for a third consecutive term. The war in Europe added another dimension to the campaign; the spectre of
military conflict hung over America. Throughout 1940 the election at home and the war in Europe dominated the newspaper
headlines and occupied the attention of the American people.
In Wisconsin Senator Robert M. La Follette, Jr. was to
face re-election. Though but forty-five years old, Young Bob
had already spent fifteen years in the seat held by his father.
Many men, after long service in the Senate, are unceremoni-
ously relegated to private life by the voters of their states.
During the heat of the fall campaign, La Follette saw his col-
league from Arizona, Senator Henry Ashurst, who had served
in the Senate for twenty-eight years, defeated in the Democratic primary by a young judge named Ernest McFarland. This
could be a sad omen for La Follette, pessimistic throughout
1940 about the European war and about his own chances for
re-election; he knew that he was in the fight of his political
life. His Progressive party had deteriorated, and the Wiscon-

sin Republicans had experienced a dramatic resurgence. Victory, were it to come at all, would not come with the ease that he had experienced in previous years. The Presidential election and the war in Europe, however, shared the headlines; the Senate race was relegated to the inner pages of Wisconsin newspapers. Nevertheless, the outcome was vitally important. La Follette had become one of the most important and influential men in Washington, a leader of the liberal and progressive forces in the Senate.   More than that, the result of his race for re-election would determine the future course of the Progressive party of Wisconsin.

In 1940 the Progressives' survival as a separate party hung in the balance.   Their overwhelming defeat in 1938 had caused many Progressives to feel that their young party was dying.   After their massive victory in 1938 the Republicans faced 1940 with a feeling of confidence, believing that at long last they could fully humble the name La Follette. If the young Progressive party tasted complete defeat for the second consecutive election, it seems likely that the blow would prove fatal.   Philip La Follette, undoubtedly the most important Progressive until his defeat in 1938, had removed himself from the scene.   Senator La Follette had been thrust into the lead, and his campaign for re-election was the most important task facing the party.   He had proven to be a more potent vote-getter than his younger brother, and as a United States Senator he now held a more important office than any other Progressive. Should all Progressive candidates for state-wide office go down to defeat, yet were La Follette to win re-election, there would still be life in the party. Should La Follette also fail, it seems doubtful that the Progressive party could have recovered from this blow.

Nineteen-forty, then, was crucial to the future of the Progressive party, and Senator Robert La Follette's re-election was its major task.   In the early part of the year, however, there was some uncertainty as to the course La Follette would follow in the coming campaign.   In April, *The Capital Times* reported the birth of a movement to support La Follette for Vice President should President Roosevelt seek re-election, but this action was not taken seriously; Senator La Follette was amused by the suggestion.   The real question was the

course La Follette would follow in his campaign for re-election
to the Senate, whether he would run as a Progressive, or whether
he would shift to one of the two major parties. If he abandoned
the party of which he was the leader, it could not hope to survive.

In late 1939 Roosevelt's Attorney General, Frank Murphy,
publicly invited notable liberals, specifically Mayor La Guardia
of New York and Senator La Follette, who found their political
home outside of the Democratic party, to join the party of
Roosevelt; they would be received "with open arms."[1] The
Attorney General presumably spoke with the knowledge and
support of the President. At about the same time Thomas R.
Amlie, who urged the Farmer-Labor party in Minnesota and the
Progressive party in Wisconsin to disband and join the Democrats, sent one of the President's administrative assistants,
Lauchlin Currie, to see Senator La Follette and urge him to run
for re-election under the Democratic banner. La Follette reportedly displayed reluctance to ask the Progressive party to
consider such a course for his own sake.[2] Many Wisconsin
Democrats, restive in their new role as the third party in a
three party state, sought their salvation in the union of the
Progressives with the Democrats. Gustave J. Keller, the Democratic nominee for Wisconsin Attorney General in 1940, reported that he tried to effect such a union:

> On August 19, 1940, speaking at Scandinavia, as
> President of the Democratic Party Organization of
> Wisconsin, "to eliminate division in the liberal ranks,
> and to form a united, solid front against the people's
> enemy—reaction," I called upon Robert M. La Fol-
> lette "to come over to the Democratic party, the party
> of Roosevelt, to carry on to victory the battle of the
> common people."[3]

Even the Democratic state chairman, Thomas R. King, went to
Washington in an attempt to persuade La Follette to run as a
Democrat.[4]

Among Progressives there was little desire to become
Democrats, but there was some sentiment for a return to the
Republican party, where, after all, "Old Bob" had waged his
holy crusades for forty-five years. Progressive state Senator

Allen J. Busby expressed the sentiment of some party members when he decided to run for re-election in the Republican party, saying that "liberals have designated it as their instrument for future political action."[5] Orland Loomis, Progressive Attorney General from 1937 to 1939, and a candidate for the Progressive gubernatorial nomination in 1940, talked with Senator La Follette about what party label Bob would run on in 1940. Loomis may have felt it best for the Progressives to return *en masse* to the Republican party.[6] La Follette privately expressed apprehension at the difficulty he would have in winning re-election as a Progressive.[7]

That Robert M. La Follette, Jr. would never have chosen politics for a career was never more apparent than after his brother's overwhelming defeat in 1938. Phil's defeat thrust the leadership of the Progressive party into Bob's hands, but he was not eager to assume the task. Despite his new role he did not take an active part in party affairs. The Progressive state chairman has recalled that most of the party's business was done without consulting the Senator; he was contacted only on major problems.[8] La Follette preferred the life in Washington, where he faced the substantial issues of national policy, to the petty politics of Wisconsin. He remained in Washington longer in the autumn than many of his associates believed that he should have done for his own sake. He did not even address the Progressive party platform convention in the fall. "As you know, I am a candidate for re-election to the United States Senate this year," he said in a form letter to Wisconsin Progressives, "but it is my duty to stay on the job in Washington."[9]

Yet, no matter how emphatically Senator La Follette disclaimed any desire to lead the Wisconsin Progressives, it would have been difficult for any one else to assume the task as long as a La Follette remained politically active. Bob knew that he could direct the Progressive party to disband and enter another party, yet this would have required a great amount of effort and persuasion, and it would have displeased some political associates in Wisconsin, most of all, his brother. Such action would have required far more time and effort than to decide simply to keep the party alive. To run for re-election as a Progressive was the easiest decision for Senator La Follette to make.

The Progressive party planned a celebration for Sunday, May 19, 1940, the sixth anniversary of its birth, in the small town of Wisconsin Rapids. Senator La Follette was to deliver the principal speech. A few days before the meeting, *The Capital Times* reported that "Sen. La Follette has informed the arrangements committee that he intends to encounter 'head-on' all rumors that he plans to run on the Democratic or Republican instead of the Progressive ticket."[10] On Saturday, May 18, La Follette participated in a party leadership conference. He declared that Progressives had an excellent chance of returning to office in 1940, but this success would depend upon organization down to every precinct.[11] The next day sixteen hundred Progressives joined in the birthday festivities. Senator La Follette spoke to the gathering about the economic problems which still confronted the nation, and of the necessity of increasing mass purchasing power. The Progressives cheered, for they all could agree with this. They had really come to hear Young Bob speak of politics, of the future of their party, and he did not disappoint them:

> On this sixth anniversary of its establishment in our state, I can say to you with a great deal of pride that the Progressive party is the party of today in Wisconsin, and I confidently believe that it will be the party of tomorrow in the nation.
>
> Reactionaries have speculated as to my political course in the coming campaign.
>
> My answer to all such speculation is that I did not join in the formation of the Progressive party in 1934 as a political expedient. I gave my whole-hearted support to this movement for a new political alignment in state and nation because I believe it is essential to a dynamic functioning of our democracy. *So far as I am concerned, the fight in Wisconsin will be waged under the banner of the Progressive party in 1940.*[12]

The Progressive party would remain in the field in 1940, and Senator Robert M. La Follette, Jr. would head the ticket.

The Wisconsin Republicans faced 1940 fully confident of

victory. They controlled the entire state government and they held a majority in both houses of the legislature. In 1936 the Republicans had failed to elect a man to the United States Congress; after the 1938 elections they held eight of ten House seats and one Senate seat. The Republicans had shaken off the lethargy of the mid-1930's and become aggressive once more; furthermore they had a smoothly working and well-financed state organization. In 1940 the Republicans throughout the nation believed that they would make heavy inroads in the huge Democratic vote of four years earlier. This Republican revival across the nation had come full-tide into Wisconsin.

The Republican upsurge throughout the nation and in Wisconsin, and the tempting prize of a seat in the United States Senate, encouraged seven Republicans to enter the Senatorial primary. Fred H. Clausen, a farm-implement manufacturer, who was called "possibly the most hard-bitten conservative that will enter the race"[13] announced his candidacy in May. His campaign was primarily an attack upon the New Deal; at one point he said, very simply, that we need men in Congress to "curb the New Deal."[14] Five other Republicans entered the race in the next three months. Just prior to the final filing date in early August a seventh candidate entered the primary. He was the former President of the University of Wisconsin, Dr. Glenn Frank.

Glenn Frank had become President of the University of Wisconsin in the summer of 1925, at the same time that Young Bob La Follette first ran for the Senate. On the evening of September 14, 1925, the night before the primary, Young Bob gave his concluding speech at the University Stock Pavilion. *The Capital Times* reported that "President Glenn Frank of the university, accompanied by Mrs. Frank . . . took seats among those occupying chairs in the 'show ring' on the ground floor of the pavilion."[15] This may have been an appropriate appearance for a new University President, yet Frank was never identified as a La Follette man.

In March, 1936, a correspondent close to the Wisconsin scene reported that "rumors" President Frank was out of favor with the La Follettes were increasing:[16] a clash between the University President and the Governor was drawing near. On

January 7, 1937, the Board of Regents of the University climaxed this struggle by voting, eight to seven, not to renew
President Frank's contract; seven of the eight regents voting
against Dr. Frank had been appointed by Governor La Follette.
The Frank case may have been, as Elmer Davis said, "the most
widely publicized episode of Phil's governorship."[17] In all the
publicity which followed, Frank probably came off more favor-
ably than La Follette; it was easier for him to point to his
dismissal as an unjustified and vindictive act than for the
Governor to review the Frank administration in an attempt to
substantiate a case against the University President. In a
bitter statement Glenn Frank claimed, probably correctly, that
the La Follette family had always opposed him. He went on
to charge that on the day in 1925 when he had been elected
University President, "George Middleton, husband of Fola La
Follette, said to me that I should not accept it, for, as he put
it, 'That is not the family's wishes.'"[18] George Middleton
immediately denied Frank's charge, and Frank disputed Middleton's denial. After Governor La Follette was defeated in November, 1938, Frank expressed his satisfaction and said: "It
is common knowledge in state and nation, that Governor La
Follette and his brother, Senator La Follette, personally ordered
and personally engineered my summary dismissal from the
presidency of the University of Wisconsin."[19]

Of the seven Republican Senatorial candidates, Frank was
the most bitterly anti-La Follette. Six days before the primary
he told a Milwaukee audience:

> The insistence of thousands of Wisconsin citizens
> finally convinced me that I am the one man in Wis-
> consin who can, once and for all, sweep the state
> clean of the last vestige of second generation La
> Folletteism.
> This La Folletteism, under the two boys, has de-
> generated into a bogus liberalism which, despite its
> shouting of all the old war cries, is at heart fascist.[20]

Two days earlier, in Appleton, Frank related that he had "felt
the heavy fist of La Follette dictatorship" and pledged that he
would "leave no stone unturned to rid Wisconsin forever of
this latter-day La Folletteism."[21] On the Friday before the

September 17 primary, Frank declared that the issue in the Senate race is "whether Wisconsin is to be freed from second generation La Folletteism which has degenerated from a Progressive movement into nothing more than a campaign year machine for landing jobs for two boys. . . . The La Follettes don't want me nominated because I know them, their motives and their methods as no other senatorial candidate does."[22] Try the Glenn Frank eradicator, especially suited to remove any and all La Follettes, available at your local precinct on Tuesday, September 17. Frank went on to point out that the La Follettes do not have a monopoly of these sins; the New Deal is also guilty of them. "Both the La Follettes and the New Deal leadership have been intolerant and vindictive. . . . They have split Wisconsin and the nation into a lot of warring groups and have sought to convince these groups that their interests are in conflict."[23] Both the La Follettes and the New Deal must be replaced. "This latter day La Folletteism is just a vest pocket edition of the thinly disguised Caesarism of the New Deal. It is therefore just as imperative to fumigate Wisconsin of this local-Hitlerism masquerading as democracy as to rid the nation of New Dealism."[24]

The five other Republicans valiantly called attention to their candidacies, but less attention was given them than to Clausen and Frank. One of the other candidates, William C. Maas (who ran a poor fifth in the primary) asserted that he was better qualified to beat La Follette than the six other Republicans, especially Frank and Clausen.[25] This only dramatized their pre-eminence in the race, and emphasized the lead they held over the rest of the field. The race was clearly between Frank and Clausen, and it was close.

On Sunday, September 15, two days before the primary, Dr. Glenn Frank planned to complete a full day of campaigning with a speech at Green Bay. His son, Glenn Jr., was driving as they traveled the last weary miles at the end of an exhausting day of politics. Fifteen miles south of Green Bay, at the intersection of highways 57 and 96, their car lurched off the road, hit a huge sandpile, and rolled over several times. Dr. Frank and his son were killed. The next day this news dominated the headlines of Wisconsin newspapers, not only because Glenn Frank was such a prominent personality, but also because his death had an immediate impact on Wisconsin politics. *The Capital Times* reported that Dr. Frank "had been chosen by some political observers to win the nomination and by almost all to run second."[26] Others believed that Frank was virtually certain to win the nomination. *The Manitowoc Herald-Times* said editorially:

> There seemed little doubt that he was leading his six opponents for the Republican senatorial nomination. His death throws the race wide open. . . .
>
> The death of the former University of Wisconsin president not only changes the Republican situation, it greatly enhances the chance of Sen. La Follette for reelection.

The *Herald-Times* went on to point out that "Frank would have bothered Bob a great deal," for, among other things, "he personified the fight against the La Follettes."[27] *The Janesville Gazette* remarked that because Frank's death came "on the eve of a probable victory at the polls he is denied a seat in the U.S. Senate."[28] The chairman of the Frank Voluntary Citizen's Committee, W. T. Doar, asked for a vote of tribute for Frank in the Tuesday primary.

Whether Dr. Glenn Frank would have won the nomination had he not been killed is, of course, impossible to say. The fall campaign undoubtedly would have been different had he faced La Follette. Dr. Frank's death threw the Republican primary into a state of confusion, but when the ballots were counted Fred Clausen emerged victorious by a huge plurality. Out of 349,935 votes for all seven Republican candidates, he polled 109,293 votes, 44,519 more than his nearest rival, Dr. John Koehler; Dr. Frank finished third. The Republicans were jubilant about their 349,935 vote turnout, compared with La Follette's 144,692 votes in the Progressive primary, where he ran unopposed.[29] The La Follettes feared Clausen as a candidate more than they had feared Glenn Frank, for they believed that Frank would not have received the conservative Republican support that went to Clausen.[30] After the primary, *The Milwaukee Journal* suggested that the Republican trend of 1938 would continue unabated in 1940. Furthermore, the *Journal* said hopefully, there is little to suggest that a candidate's name (that is, La Follette) has any magic in it.[31]

Senator La Follette would have to rely on his own efforts; his party was obviously too weak to pull him through. A spirited five-man race for the gubernatorial nomination failed to attract voters to the Progressive primary. As their candidate for Governor the Progressives had sought a new leader, a replacement for Phil La Follette. "The Progressive party is now at the crossroads in Wisconsin," gubernatorial candidate Harold E. Stafford said. "We must now select a new leader of our party and it is important that the successor to Phil La Follette be able to carry on with those liberal achievements which have made Wisconsin a leader in this nation."[32] Stafford attempted to suggest himself as Phil La Follette's successor, yet in their primary the Progressives placed him second to former state Attorney General Orland S. Loomis. If anyone other than Senator La Follette were to assume the leadership of the party it would have to be the gubernatorial nominee, but Loomis failed to do so; he was neither a colorful nor a dynamic personality. Party leadership, by default, remained in Senator La Follette's hands, and the primary made the party look weaker than ever.

In 1940 the Democrats were the majority party in the United States, but the Democratic organization in Wisconsin was weak and demoralized. The existence of the Progressive party had undercut the opportunity for the Wisconsin Democrats to establish a solid foot-hold on the left flank. The Progressives also had taken much patronage and many votes which the Democrats felt should belong to them. It was no secret that the Roosevelt administration worked in harmony with Senator La Follette and rewarded his support for New Deal measures with substantial patronage. Certainly the Wisconsin Democrats were aware of this, and were upset by this "betrayal." Some Democrats had hoped to lure the Progressives, and particularly Senator La Follette, over to the Democratic party. To some, such a union would represent the union of the liberal forces in Wisconsin against the "reactionaries" who favored the entrenched special interests. To others such a union would simply mean that the state Democrats might win elections, and that they could establish relations with the Roosevelt administration. These efforts proved unsuccessful. In 1940 the Wisconsin Democratic party, sacrificed in the coalition of 1938, and ignored by its national leader, was the weakest of the three parties. Former state Attorney General James E. Finnegan won the Democratic nomination for United States Senator, but this seemed a dubious distinction. Finnegan had opposed Roosevelt for a third term, and was labeled an "anti-New Dealer." Furthermore, the Democrats received only twenty-one per cent of the total primary vote. Finnegan seemed safely out of the race; the election for Senator was clearly between Clausen and La Follette.

Fred H. Clausen's campaign consisted of three major elements: first, he attacked the New Deal; second, he called for labor-management harmony; and third, he attacked Senator La Follette. In the early days of the campaign, Clausen took an adventurous plunge in favor of the good things in life by declaring that "our hopes for ourselves and our children are that the American way of life may be preserved and enlarged."[33] Thereafter his campaign took more definite shape. The New Deal has "lost control of the business of government, and they don't know what to do about it."[34] Clausen, a successful businessman himself, charged that a "blank check" appropriation of millions has been entrusted to an "amateur" who never made a success "of any important business venture."[35] The New Deal consists of many "fantastic dreams" of huge public expenditures.[36] We must abandon this reckless approach, for "we cannot be strong with a nation riding on a wave of spending and mounting national debt."[37] Clausen's solution to this unbelievable mess was to introduce "sound business principles" into the federal government. Harmony between labor and management was essential to restore the economic balance of America. "The New Deal stresses the view that industry is antagonistic to labor. This theory must be exploded for a return to prosperity."[38]

After describing the sinking ship that was the New Deal, Clausen firmly tied La Follette to the mast. He "is an apostle of discontent—working hand-in-hand with the New Dealers— he must, therefore, take his share of blame for the disastrous results of the New Deal's fantastic and unworkable theories."[39] Senator La Follette "is unfit to do the kind of job that is needed today in the United States senate. His record, extending over 15 years, is negative and his ideas of government will not restore jobs to a single man in private industry. He is heart and soul a New Dealer."[40] Actually he is heart and soul more than a New Dealer. "The only thing Senator La Follette did not like about these impractical projects was that they didn't go far enough."[41] Clausen's basic strategy was simple: he attacked La Follette, who was for the New Deal, which was against labor-management harmony.

Clausen also attacked La Follette on one politically vulnerable point. Senator La Follette, along with approximately sixty other Congressmen, had signed a telegram in 1938 sending congratulations to the Loyalist Government of Spain on a victory over the Fascists. Because of the anti-clericalism of the Loyalist Government and the Communist support it received, this could weaken La Follette among Roman Catholic voters. La Follette did not repudiate his action. Clausen charged: "I hereby indict Senator La Follette for being false to that oath [of office] when he sent a cablegram of congratulations to the Communist government of Spain on Feb. 1, 1938."[42] Raymond Clapper, a national political correspondent favorable to La Follette, reported that this was probably the most damaging single factor in the campaign against the Senator.[43] Clausen's entire campaign was conservative and strongly anti-New Deal. At one point he looked in wonder at La Follette's campaign and said that the Senator's speeches "are devoted to attacks on the Republican state administration and to eulogies of his father, 'Old Bob' La Follette."[44] Yet, Clausen did not attack La Follette with the personal vindictiveness that had characterized Glenn Frank's primary campaign.

Senator La Follette waged a vigorous and intensive campaign in the weeks after the primary. He voiced his opposition to Roosevelt's policy toward war-torn Europe. He stood upon his own record of support for progressive legislation, and urged more federal action to strengthen a sagging economy. He vigorously attacked the state administration of Republican Governor Julius P. Heil. And, he faced a perplexing dilemma in trying to decide who, if anyone, he should support in the Presidential election.

The warm relationship between President Roosevelt and Senator La Follette, upset by Phil La Follette's National Progressives of America, was shaken still further by the outbreak of war in Europe. President Roosevelt believed that it was more important for the United States to assure a British victory over Germany than for the United States to remain out of the war. Senator La Follette believed that it was more important for the United States to remain out of the war than to assure a British victory. La Follette's opposition to Roosevelt's foreign policy placed him in the uncomfortable company of Senator Alexander Wiley and the Wisconsin Republican Congressmen. He opposed any reductions in the trade restrictions contained in the embargo act. He opposed peacetime conscription. He opposed the deal which gave Great Britain fifty old-age destroyers in exchange for military bases in the Western Hemisphere. At all costs, La Follette wanted to keep America out of the war. He was afraid that support for England would lead directly to our own military involvement. The first casualty of our entry into a European war, La Follette claimed, would be "the democratic form of government."[45] The alternative to the present policies, upon which both Presidential candidates are agreed, is "to rebuild our defenses until America shall be impregnable to attack by any or all nations of the world."[46] Democracy is threatened in the world as never before. "Modern war cannot be fought under Democratic control. It requires dictatorship for total war."[47] We must put our own house in order so that our democracy will not rot from within. "We have seen democracies fall, not so much because they failed in a military sense but because they failed to make democracy work."[48] While war rages abroad and while "we remain at peace, we can act to strengthen America internally by putting our human and material resources to work."[49] Our national defense "requires just as much a nation and a people whose social economic and spiritual house is in order. And ours is not."[50] On the Friday before the election, La Follette summed up his position on the war:

> We have two objectives. First, we must rearm America so that we shall be invincible against attack by any or all nations. Second, we must learn the lesson taught by France's collapse, that our economy and our people constitute a domestic front as important as our military front.[51]

La Follette emphasized foreign policy in his speeches before the campaign began in earnest. After the primary he mentioned it less often, putting the major emphasis of his campaign on the issues with which he had been associated throughout his career—social and welfare legislation and economic security.

Senator La Follette discussed at great length domestic progressive legislation. In a radio speech criticizing the Roosevelt foreign policy, he also said:

> Here in America agriculture is entering the third decade of depression. Ten million men remain unemployed. The needy aged struggle along with a pittance which decries self-respect. And youth, the nation's most precious asset, has little to look forward to beyond enforced service in the army.[52]

Present social and welfare legislation is a step in the right direction, but it does not go far enough. Present old-age pensions are inadequate. The present tax system is unfair. "In place of these unjust taxes, we must enact income and inheritance taxes based upon the progressive principle of taxation according to ability to pay."[53] The federal food stamp program should be expanded. Farmers need more federal assistance to struggle out of the agricultural depression. Organized labor needs the support of the federal government in its quest for its legitimate objectives. "A strong, alert and intelligent labor movement is necessary to America's internal and external security. The Wisconsin reactionaries now in power have done their utmost to set the farmer against labor and labor against the farmer, so they could rule triumphantly over both."[54] The war in Europe should not tax our energies when we have so many unsolved problems here at home. "We have the world's greatest capacity to produce. It is in the field of distribution and the control of money and credit that our economic system has failed to function at full capacity. . . . It is obvious that our economic system is lagging and weak."[55]

Senator La Follette so sharply attacked the administration of Republican Governor Julius P. Heil that it often seemed as though he were running for Governor. Indeed, one close observer insisted that La Follette was more vigorous in his attacks on Heil than was the Progressive gubernatorial nominee,

Orland Loomis.[56] The administration received censure for its
"flagrant violation of solemn economy promises, its broken
promises, extravagant operation of the state government and
deliberate wrecking of many state agencies set up to benefit
the people. . . . it was this kind of irresponsible government
that causes the peoples of Europe to lose faith in the democracies . . . If any administration ever deserved to be rebuked
at the polls and driven from office, this is it."[57]   La Follette
attacked Heil for favoring repeal of the tax on oleomargarine,
a powerful issue in the dairy state.   It was an administration
of "reactionary Big Business."[58]   A sales tax would be in effect by July 1, 1941, if the "reactionary, Milwaukee Athletic
Club branch of the Republican party" is returned to power.[59]
In short, the Heil administration "has given Wisconsin the
largest budget, the biggest tax levy, the biggest pay roll and
the biggest deficit in the history of the state."[60]   Perhaps La
Follette attacked the Heil administration so vigorously because he believed it was unpopular; in the Republican primary,
an unknown candidate, Dr. James Robinson, polled half as
many votes as Heil. Julius Heil was also the culprit who had
defeated his brother two years before.

If La Follette had few kind words for Heil, he had few
words of any sort for his own opponent, Fred Clausen. In Milwaukee on October 22, La Follette characterized the election
as a battle "between organized wealth and the people."

> Here in Wisconsin the Republican ticket is domi-
> nated by a man running for governor who made his
> millions in war profits during the last war and by a
> man running for United States senator who made his
> fortune selling machinery for farmers at tremendous
> profits.[61]

This was as close as La Follette ever came to mentioning his
opponent.

One of the mysteries of the early fall was what Roosevelt
and La Follette would do about each other.   La Follette had
supported the President in 1932 and 1936, and Roosevelt had
indirectly endorsed the Senator in 1934.   Yet, the increasing
crescendo of La Follette's attacks on the President's foreign
policy cast strong doubt that either man could support the

other in 1940.   On September 11 La Follette delivered a radio
speech from Washington under the sponsorship of the America
First Committee.   He attacked the Roosevelt foreign policy in
general for "going down the same road as we took in 1916—17,"
and, in particular, for the recent Destroyers-for-Bases deal.
La Follette continued:

> The two old parties have evaded this momentous
> issue in their platforms.   Their presidential candi-
> dates see eye to eye on foreign policy.   This de-
> prives the people of an effective choice in the presi-
> dential campaign on the supreme issue.[62]

La Follette's strong opposition to the foreign policies favored
by both Presidential candidates might prevent him from endorsing either one.   Certainly La Follette had no intention of
endorsing Wendell Willkie; the only question was whether La
Follette would support Roosevelt or whether he would remain
neutral. This proved to be a difficult decision for the Senator,
for he had many reservations about either course.[63]

Aside from his opposition to the President on foreign affairs, La Follette would face an embarrassing political dilemma
if he decided to support Roosevelt for a third term.   In the
summer of 1927 President Calvin Coolidge chose not to run.
Senator La Follette did not usually find himself in agreement
with Coolidge, yet he could not help but feel that here the
President had made a wonderfully wise choice.   A number of
months earlier, on George Washington's birthday, La Follette
had introduced a resolution which declared that it was "the
sense of the Senate" that a two-term limitation for a President had become "a part of our republican system of Government," and that a third term for any President "would be unwise, unpatriotic and frought with peril to our free institutions."[64]   "Calvin Coolidge gives every indication of being
an active and aggressive candidate for a third term as President of the United States," La Follette said later.   "The intelligent citizens of this country know that once a President
has smashed the third-term precedent, there will be no effective limit to the tenure of a Chief Executive who has come to
exert kingly power, which gives an unscrupulous man an opportunity to perpetuate himself in office."[65]   "Students of

politics, both American and foreign, properly regard the President of the United States as the most powerful individual in the world," La Follette told the Senate in early 1928. "Establishment of the precedent that one man may continue to wield this power for longer than eight years would mark a definite step toward the abrogation of popular government."[66] Perhaps no stronger statements against a third term for the President can be found. The La Follette resolution passed the Senate on February 10, 1928. The words which La Follette uttered with such force and emphasis in 1927 and 1928 now came to haunt him as he contemplated supporting Franklin D. Roosevelt for a third term in 1940.

Twelve days after the September primary, as he prepared to begin his campaign, Senator La Follette endorsed President Roosevelt for re-election and said:

> I have searched my mind and heart. I have not been unmindful of the fact that I sponsored an anti-third term resolution in the days of the false prosperity of President Coolidge. But for myself, choosing between the two presidential candidates in this critical period, I can come to only one conclusion.[67]

The next day La Follette added: "On the record as made by the candidates for President, the American way of life has a better opportunity of working out its destiny in the next four years under the administration of Franklin D. Roosevelt." La Follette added that he made this decision "regardless of the political consequences to myself."[68]

On an ideological basis alone, La Follette's support of the President seemed perfectly reasonable and understandable. Both Roosevelt and Willkie saw eye to eye on foreign policy, so they were equally bad on that score. Yet domestic issues were another matter; here the President's record was far superior. "If we get into this war," La Follette told his secretary Norman Clapp, "I'd sure rather go into war under Roosevelt than under Willkie." La Follette believed that in a war situation Roosevelt was more likely to preserve the domestic accomplishments of the New Deal.[69] Furthermore, his support of the President would doubtless have a political effect, and La Follette was well aware of this. When he spoke before a gathering sponsored by the Amalgamated Clothing Workers of America (C.I.O.) he drew his most enthusiastic applause when he repeated his endorsement of Roosevelt.[70] He repeated his support for the President throughout the campaign. On election eve he stated that he was "still for the third term tradition." Nevertheless, "I'd rather break the third term precedent than turn the country over to the crowd that nearly wrecked it when they had control the last time."[71]

The Republicans believed that La Follette's endorsement of the President might backfire, and they tried to encourage this reaction. Clausen recalled La Follette's anti-third term resolution of 1928 and repeatedly hammered at his endorsement of Roosevelt as hypocritical and based on pure political expediency. *The Milwaukee Journal* recalled his 1928 resolution, and said that he had been "talking about *any* president who sought a third term. . . . What a cheap performance it is! Even New Deal Democrats ought to resent this palpable effort to garner votes from them."[72]

Senator La Follette's support for the President had an important bearing on his own campaign for re-election. Four prominent Democrats came to Wisconsin and spoke in his behalf. Attorney General Robert H. Jackson and Senators Sheridan Downey of California and Robert Wagner of New York all urged his re-election. Whatever effect these visits may have had, certainly they appear insignificant compared with the fourth prominent Democrat who came to Wisconsin—Henry A. Wallace, the Democratic Vice Presidential nominee.

The Democratic party in Wisconsin was not only weak and demoralized and without hope of victory but, on the Senate race, it was badly split. The core of the Democratic state organization, the conservative politicians of the 1930's, wanted to support the Democratic nominee, James Finnegan, out of party loyalty and sheer force of habit. Yet many leading Wisconsin Democrats did not want to support him; they regarded him as an anti-New Dealer. Shortly after the primary the Democratic national committeeman, Charles E. Broughton, wrote an editorial in his newspaper, *The Sheboygan Press*, saying that "James E. Finnegan, candidate for U.S. senate on the Democratic ticket, cannot hope for support of those who believe in the policies of President Roosevelt."[73] Broughton

left no doubt that a Roosevelt Democrat must support La Follette.   Finnegan had no apparent chance of victory, and re-
signed himself to his fate.   In the middle of October, while
Clausen and La Follette were traversing the state in vigorous
campaigns, Finnegan said: "I have never had any intention of
withdrawing."   Almost as an afterthought, he added: "Moreover, I'll make a campaign."[74]   Six days later, Finnegan announced that he was "whole-heartedly behind President Roosevelt in his efforts to be re-elected to the presidency in November. . . . I am 100% in accord with President Roosevelt's foreign
policy."[75] These words no doubt pleased Clausen; Finnegan's
activity might draw some votes that otherwise would have
gone to La Follette. Yet his endorsement of the President came
too late and too reluctantly to please liberal Democrats, who
still recalled that he had opposed much of the New Deal domestic program.   The Democrats, then, had a senatorial candidate who apparently had no chance for victory, and who had
endorsed President Roosevelt at the last moment.

Democratic Vice Presidential nominee Henry A. Wallace
was scheduled to speak in Madison on October 22.   His remarks would reflect the position of the administration.   In
1934 La Follette had received Roosevelt's blessing; would the
administration say kind words about La Follette again, or
would it support the Democrat Finnegan, or would Wallace
simply ignore Wisconsin politics and preach against sin on
the national level? Three days before Wallace was scheduled
to come to Wisconsin twenty-two prominent Democrats, including their gubernatorial nominee Francis McGovern (who
had become a Roosevelt Democrat in 1934), sent Wallace a
telegram urging him to endorse the entire Democratic state
ticket, and, specifically, James E. Finnegan. Some of the sign-
ers threatened to boycott the Madison rally unless Wallace did
so.[76] The day before Wallace's appearance, *The Milwaukee
Journal* reported that Wallace apparently would name no names
in state contests, either Democrats or Progressives.[77]

The stage was set for Wallace's speech in Madison on
October 22. He joggled the crowd and upset many of the Democrats with his very first words:

It is a pleasure to be with you here in Wisconsin,
a state famous for its long record of liberal legisla-

tion, and for its liberal influence on the rest of the United States. I desire on this occasion particularly to express my appreciation of the untiring support we in Washington have received from Democratic and Progressive congressmen in Wisconsin and from your senior senator, Robert M. La Follette.

In protest, McGovern, Gustave Keller, and Finnegan walked off the speaker's platform and out of the rally. Charles E. Broughton and state chairman King applauded Wallace's remarks.[78] The split was now complete. Wallace's statement, *The New York Times* reported, had been made "after consultation with the White House, [and] was seen as completing an alliance between the Democratic national organization and the Wisconsin State Progressive organization."[79] Undaunted, Finnegan began to sound like a candidate. On the Friday before election, he said that "a vote for La Follette is a vote to destroy the democratic party in this state."[80]

Senator La Follette hoped that his support of Roosevelt, and the President's kind words for him, would aid his campaign. John Burnham of *The Waupaca County Herald* told Orland Loomis that "Bob's nod to F.D.R. is considered a smart move up here in the sticks."[81] Maurice B. Pasch, Loomis's campaign manager, remarked that if "it is really for Roosevelt as it now looks, then I am satisfied that we have better than a fighting chance to win."[82] Many Progressives, like Pasch, saw a close correlation between the Progressive strength and the Roosevelt strength. La Follette hoped that he could ride the Roosevelt coat-tails to victory. On the other hand, were the President to lose Wisconsin he could carry La Follette to defeat.

A report in *The New York Times* said that "Senator La Follette's friends will tell you that one of the greatest obstacles he is facing now is of his own making in declaring for Mr. Roosevelt and a third term [because of] the general anti-administration trend which they, along with most others, detect in Wisconsin."[83] More than that, the Republicans hoped that the President's apparent support of La Follette would backfire, so enraging Wisconsin Democrats that they would take the drastic action of voting Republican. *The Milwaukee Jour—*

nal counseled Wisconsin Democrats to "show their disapproval
of the betrayal of the Democratic party to the La Follette privately owned family party by voting for Clausen for Senator."
Indeed they could make their disapproval complete by voting
for Willkie.[84]

Organized labor supported Senator La Follette in 1940.
Even before the primary the Wisconsin C.I.O. endorsed the
Senator as one of the "nationally prominent friends of labor."
The C.I.O. went on to say:

> Wheeler and La Follette have distinguished them-
> selves as leading spokesmen against the increasing
> U.S. drift to war. The Wisconsin Senator gained wide-
> spread labor popularity through his chairmanship of
> the epoch-making Senate Civil Liberties Committee,
> whose investigations focused public attention on anti
> democratic processes of tory employers.[85]

For only a few months longer would La Follette hear such warm
words of praise from the Wisconsin C.I.O. The railroad brotherhoods also endorsed the Senator. Fifty Wisconsin labor leaders
formed "Labor's Committee for Roosevelt, La Follette, and
Loomis."[86]   Since 1936 the Socialists in Wisconsin had supported the Progressives, and Daniel W. Hoan, former Socialist
mayor of Milwaukee, said: "If this state cares anything about
its reputation in this nation it will send young Bob back to the
U.S. senate. Anyone choosing three or four of the biggest men
in the senate would have to name Bob."[87]

Two days before the election Edward P. Curry, the Democratic leader in Milwaukee County, issued a statement on behalf of the county committee which he quite candidly described
as "drastic."   The only way to defeat La Follette "and return
good government to Wisconsin," Curry said, is for Democrats
to unite on Republican Clausen. "For six long years the Democratic party of Wisconsin has been sabotaged and betrayed for
the sole benefit of the brothers La Follette."   Curry pointed
out that the Progressives enjoy "the undivided support of
labor," and that "the brothers La Follette absolutely control
many labor leaders." At least these labor leaders do not support the Democrats.

We believe that good government can only be returned to this state by defeating the Progressive party,
which is truly the party of confusion and double deal-
ing. The only practical way we know to accomplish
that end is to defeat Dictator La Follette for re-election to the United States senate and retire him per-
manently to his palatial estate in the great dominion
state of Virginia.

We fully realize that we recommend very drastic
action, but we sincerely feel that such drastic action
is necessary at this time, and fully justified in order
to make possible the re-establishment of the Democratic party in its proper place of prestige. The truly
American way is the two party way—Democrat and
Republican.[88]

Curry saw very clearly that with La Follette's defeat the Progressive party would die. The Democrats stood to gain more
from its demise than the Republicans. The rural Progressives
of Old Bob's day had added an urban pillar to their strength;
if their party died these urban Progressives probably would
drift over to the Democratic party. Most Progressives supported President Roosevelt in 1940 as they did four years
earlier. In 1936, while Roosevelt won a record vote in Wisconsin the state Democrats finished third. The same story
probably would repeat for the Democrats in 1940: the race in
Wisconsin between Roosevelt and Willkie would be close, yet
the state Democrats figured to finish far behind the Republicans and the Progressives. With the death of the Progressive
party in 1940 the Wisconsin Democrats could rebound, and
perhaps by 1942 they could offer a serious threat to the Republicans. La Follette's defeat was the key to the death of
the Progressive party. These were probably the thoughts which
prompted Curry to issue his statement.

Virtually all observers forecast that the Senate race would
be close. La Follette's position on the European war probably
helped him more than it harmed him. The Wisconsin delegation to Congress had presented a united front against Roosevelt's policies. Furthermore, it would not appear to be terribly unpopular for La Follette to vow to the mothers of the

state that he would never vote to send their sons to die on
foreign battlefields. One reporter said that La Follette "con-
siders his stand on foreign policy his strongest point for re-
election, even though he disagreed with the president. The
rest of the way, as strategy goes, he is a Roosevelt New
Dealer."[89] Another observer entered a contrary view; he felt
that La Follette's votes in the Senate on the European war
"may not be popular."[90] La Follette had based most of his campaign on the issues of economic security and social welfare
legislation, the domestic issues with which he had been associated. Moreover, he could look back upon two primary and
three general election contests which he had won overwhelmingly. Never before had he seriously been threatened. Yet,
after forty years of political dominance in Wisconsin, the formidable name La Follette faced the imminent threat of final defeat.

Senator La Follette's peril drew national attention to his
campaign. Raymond Clapper wrote that Senator La Follette
"among Washington newspaper correspondents is ranked near
the top in ability and . . . would be a credit to any state." Yet,
Clapper wrote, La Follette was in danger of losing.[91] Drew
Pearson and Robert S. Allen paid tribute to La Follette as an
"able, courageous, conscientious son of the late great progressive," but "this year the famous crusading dynasty is in
real danger of being unseated."[92]

On the Sunday before the election a rally in Milwaukee
heard Senator Robert F. Wagner of New York extol the merits
of Senator La Follette. "Bob La Follette is not a member of
my party, but that does not deter me," Senator Wagner said,
"because his patriotism, integrity and brilliant capacity for
public service transcend all party lines. He has vindicated
his heritage. He has indeed proved himself an illustrious son
of an illustrious sire."[93] This meeting was so successful and
evoked so much enthusiasm that it raised the confidence in
La Follette's camp of the Senator's chances for victory.[94] The
next night, on the eve of the election, La Follette said that he
was fully aware that he faced the hardest battle of his political career. He charged that "organized wealth" and the "special interests" were spending more to defeat him than had
ever been spent in a Wisconsin election. He added:

> This is no innocent advertising campaign, but a bid for power by special interests who desire to seize control of government for selfish purposes. I have incurred powerful enemies in my 15 years in the senate and am proud of it. My enemies have moved in to defeat me if money can do it. I can't fight them with money but can only depend on the loyalty of the voters. The people on Tuesday will give their answer to the special interests bidding for power in the state and nation.[95]

La Follette defended himself and his record. "I'm human, I've made mistakes," he said, "but I wouldn't trade my record in the United States senate with any senator now living."[96]

On the morning of the election, La Follette told his secretary Norman Clapp that he believed he would lose. The Clapps were going to be at the Maple Bluff farm in the evening to listen to the returns, and La Follette did not want anyone to make a fuss or feel sorry for him if he were defeated.[97] Election night promised to provide much high tension and drama. The slow counting of ballots produces an atmosphere much like a race, in which the lead often changes and the identity of the winner frequently remains in doubt down to the wire. The race is fictitious, for the ballots have all been cast before the counting really begins, but the semblance of a race is very real. At midnight, the returns showed La Follette ahead by 15,000 votes. Two hours later the lead had shifted and Clausen led by 6,000 votes. At 8:00 A.M. La Follette forged into the lead for good.[98]

Robert M. La Follette, Jr. defeated Fred H. Clausen by just over 50,000 votes. Out of a total of 1,338,135 votes, La Follette received 605,609 votes, Clausen 553,692 votes, and Finnegan 176,688 votes. The Presidential race in Wisconsin was even closer, but President Roosevelt carried the state 704,821 to 679,206 votes. Heil was re-elected Governor, but by a margin of less than 13,000 votes over Loomis. Devotees of the virtues of non-partisanship could rejoice that Wisconsin parceled out a victory to each of the three parties in the three major contests. Of these three state races La Follette won with the largest plurality. He hit his stride with a 54,820

vote margin in Milwaukee county and a 20,973 vote margin in
Dane county, the two most populous counties in the state. Yet,
Roosevelt carried the industrial counties of Kenosha, Racine,
and Milwaukee by wider margins than did La Follette. La Follette carried the rural and traditionally Progressive western
part of Wisconsin by a larger margin than did the President.
Though both men generally ran well in the same areas and both
ran poorly in the same areas, La Follette's victory rested on a
base more rural and less urban and industrial than the President's. It was largely a personal victory for both La Follette
and Roosevelt in Wisconsin, for the Republicans extended
their grip on other state offices and added to their majorities
in the state legislature. Republicans, with the exception of
Governor Heil, won their state-wide offices by impressive
majorities. Finnegan ran from 60,000 to 100,000 behind the
rest of the Democratic state ticket; many New Deal supporters
voted a straight Democratic ticket except for United States
Senator.[99]

One La Follette partisan could not contain his joy at the
Senator's victory. "The thing that makes us feel like throw-
ing our hat into the air is the fact that having won the toughest
election of his career, Wisconsin will now have Bob in the
senate as long as he lives and desires to retain his office."[100]
This enthusiasm may have been premature, but it was understandable. Robert M. La Follette, Jr. had just won the most
difficult battle of his political career. The Progressive party
won no state-wide offices and actually lost thirteen of its
forty-two seats in the state Legislature. Nevertheless, the
Progressive party was still alive. Progressives were unanimous in stating that La Follette's victory had been their major
concern. Harold E. Stafford had concluded a campaign letter
in behalf of his own quest for the Progressive gubernatorial
nomination with these words:

> It is extremely important that Bob La Follette be
> returned to the U.S. Senate. I urge you to do every-
> thing within your power to secure his re-election as
> that is probably the most important contest now fac-
> ing us.[101]

Orland S. Loomis, the unsuccessful Progressive nominee for

Governor, wrote to Senator La Follette's secretary one month after the election:

> To my mind, the election of Bob was more impor-
> tant than that of a Governor. Had Bob been defeated,
> everyone would have said that the Progressive move-
> ment would be dead for some time. With his re-elec-
> tion, they all know and understand that the Progres-
> sive movement is a live and vital force.[102]

Robert M. La Follette, Jr. was one of the chief architects in the formation of the Progressive party. Even though his brother was the dominant leader while Governor, Bob proved to be the better vote-getter. Were this greatest of all Progressive vote-getters, with the legendary name of La Follette, to face defeat the Progressives would be without a state-wide office-holder. Furthermore, the Progressives simply could not secure another candidate with the vote-getting ability that Young Bob La Follette possessed. Senator La Follette's defeat would have left the Progressive party completely demoralized; his victory kept the party alive.

During the campaign La Follette did not provide any leadership or direction to the party's over-all campaign. He kept his own campaign separate from Loomis's gubernatorial bid. After the election Otto Christenson, the defeated Progressive nominee for state Attorney General, wrote to Loomis:

> I am also thoroughly convinced that if Bob had re-
> turned just one week earlier from Congress—and I
> do not believe his presence at Washington was in-
> dispensable the last week he was there, or that he
> would have been criticized if he had left a week
> earlier, that one extra week's campaigning on his
> part, in which he could have spent at least 18 cam-
> paign addresses in 9 extra counties, would have been
> enough to have carried you in.[103]

Dissatisfaction with Senator La Follette's lack of leadership was expressed by his own loyal followers.

With his Senate seat secure for six years, and with the increasing American drift to war, Wisconsin politics were of no immediate concern to Senator La Follette. Yet, his own

future political course and the future course of the Progressive party were inseparably allied. With La Follette's victory
as its only major accomplishment, the continued separate existence of the Progressive party remained open to question.
In the weeks after the election, some Wisconsin Democrats
made overtures toward a possible Democratic-Progressive coalition. One of them, Charles E. Broughton, urged a coalition
of all the liberal forces in the state and added that "Senator
La Follette belongs in the democratic party because he is a
liberal."[104] The unsuccessful Progressive candidate for Governor, Orland Loomis, took solace in the fact that he lost by
a razor-thin margin and gave an interested ear to the proposals
for a possible coalition. Nevertheless, the future destiny of
the Progressive party clearly lay in the hands of its unwilling
leader, Senator Robert M. La Follette, Jr.

Chapter IV

THE PROGRESSIVE PARTY DURING THE WAR

In the 1940 election only Senator Robert M. La Follette's re-election had provided the Progressive party's margin of survival. Yet, the six-year old party was at its lowest ebb. It had failed to elect a Governor. It had lost thirteen places in the state Legislature. In addition to this decline in its strength, the Progressive party was now deeply divided.

War raged in Europe and threatened to engulf the United States—this one fact dominated the news. President Roosevelt attempted to grant Great Britain all possible material support, deeming her victory essential to the security of the United States. Shortly after his re-election the President presented his Lend-Lease program to Congress, whereby the United States would lend huge quantities of war materials to England. This program aroused bitter opposition and added to the fear that the President's policies were leading the United States into a war which did not involve her vital interests. Roosevelt's opponents countered that the United States would better be served if it pursued a policy of strict "non-intervention" in the affairs of Europe. There were many shades of opinion on both sides of this question. The general issue of "isolation" or "intervention" disrupted normal political patterns and cut across party lines. The two national parties were, by their nature, large, unweildy coalitions of various groups, fully familiar with factional divisions. The recent campaign had demonstrated their ability to submerge embarrassing differences within their ranks. They could endure a

split such as this, certainly with much less strain than a generally unified, localized one-state party. It was this issue of
foreign policy which so seriously split the Progressive party
of Wisconsin.

The La Follette brothers vehemently opposed Roosevelt's
foreign policy. Phil La Follette continued his nationwide cru-
sade against any American intervention, however indirect, in
the European war. Bob La Follette, from his podium in the Senate, also voiced his opposition to the major Roosevelt policies.
In September, 1941, Bob asserted that both Roosevelt and Willkie had broken their promises to keep the United States out of
the war, and that Roosevelt was "circuiting the constitutional
power of congress to declare war" in ordering the Navy to
shoot Axis warships on sight. La Follette felt that the question of active involvement in the war would force a political
realignment in 1942, and he urged those "opposed to entering
this war to mobilize for the political battles which lie just
ahead."[1] A month later, on the floor of the Senate, La Follette
attacked a Roosevelt proposal to modify further the Neutrality
laws. He charged that this would draw the United States to
the brink of war, that, indeed, it might draw this nation beyond the point of no return. "I contend that it [war] should
be resorted to by a democratic nation only when its vital interests are at stake," La Follette said. The Senator went on
to say:

> My fear is that after this nation shall have poured
> out its lifeblood and its treasury in a catastrophic
> conflict, instead of establishing the "four freedoms"
> we shall be forced, as will the leaders of every other
> country, into a gigantic program of imperialism and
> exploitation. Then we shall have to police the world,
> and in order to do that we shall have to maintain in
> this country a permanent military establishment on a
> conscription basis. In addition we shall have to give
> economic transfusions to the British Empire, our part-
> ner in the job of policing the world.[2]

Congressmen Hull, Sauthoff, and Gehrmann, the three Progressive members of the House of Representatives, supported
the La Follette position.

William T. Evjue, Madison's monument to crusading journalism, became the Progressives' most articulate spokesman
in support of the Roosevelt policies.   He had consistently
supported the elder La Follette, and both younger La Follettes
until the late 1930's.   He became disenchanted with Phil La
Follette during 1937, and finally split with him in 1938 because the National Progressives of America was hostile to
President Roosevelt.   The European war further divided Evjue
and the La Follette brothers, a schism which seemed beyond
repair. Evjue's *Capital Times* directed the brunt of its attack
against Phil La Follette and the isolationist America First Committee, and it supported Roosevelt's policy "to keep the war
away from the shores of the western hemisphere [by furnishing]
Great Britain with the tools with which to stay Nazi aggres-
sion."[3]   It is impossible to tell with any precision how many
Progressives supported the La Follettes and how many supported Evjue.   If the party were to take an official position,
certainly the La Follette view would prevail; still in 1941 it
would be folly for the Wisconsin Progressives to adopt a position so vehemently opposed by the La Follettes. Yet, to com-
mit the party to one side in the controversy, as the La Follette
brothers well knew, risked the alienation of much Progressive
support, a risk they were very reluctant to take. In the months
before Pearl Harbor the party did not take an official position
on the United States policy toward the European war.

The division in the Progressive party came to the surface
most clearly in July and August, 1941.   On July 8, Republican
Stephen Bolles, the First District Congressman, died. A special primary was called for August 8 and a special election
for August 29 to fill the vacant Congressional seat.   Thomas
R. Amlie, who had played a crucial role in the formation of
the Progressive party in 1934, and who had been elected to
Congress in 1934 and 1936 as a Progressive, entered the race.
In the middle 1930's Amlie had agitated for a national third
party, for, as he said:

> I believe that a change is inevitable from the
> profit motivated economy . . . to the planned produc-
> tion that will take its place, and as I see it, planned
> production cannot take place unless the Government

owns and controls the operation of that which is to
be planned.[4]

By 1941 he had subdued these economic thoughts and become
simply a Roosevelt Democrat, a supporter of the New Deal
domestic program. Of far greater importance, he gave complete support to Roosevelt's foreign policy. "Since I am in
support of the president's program, foreign as well as domestic," Amlie said, "I could not make the race for Congress on
the ticket of a party that was definitely committed to complete opposition."[5] He filed as a Democrat. Editor Evjue immediately endorsed Amlie.

There was, at first, considerable doubt what the official
course of the Progressive party would be in the special election. As we shall see, despite the European war many liberal
Democrats and Progressives desired a coalition of their forces.
Amlie's candidacy might have been a prelude to such a coalition.   Progressives who supported Evjue and Roosevelt generally supported Amlie, and they hoped that the La Follettes
would value Amlie's position on domestic matters enough to
get behind his candidacy. The question arose at a First District caucus of Progressives.   The party officially repudiated
any projected coalition by endorsing State Senator Kenneth
Greenquist, who supported the New Deal domestic program
but sided with the La Follettes on foreign policy. In his editorial for *The Progressive* Senator La Follette said that "all
liberal-minded Americans who are determined to keep this
country out of the recurring wars of the Old World, and to
solve the crucial economic and social problems here at home"
should support Greenquist.[6] La Follette later attacked Amlie's
candidacy as a Democrat as "a real attempt by Democrats of
Wisconsin to take over the Progressive party in Wisconsin
and destroy its entity."[7] La Follette's words did not sway all
Progressives.   One observer said that "the strongest men in
the La Follette ranks in the first district have united with the
Democrats in support of 'Tom' Amlie for the Democratic congressional nomination."[8] The primary on August 8 revealed
the seriousness of the Progressive split. To qualify for a
place on the ballot, a party's candidates in the primary had
to receive five per cent of the party's average vote for Gov-

ernor in the past two elections. The Progressives needed 2053
votes to qualify for a place on the ballot. Greenquist, unopposed for the Progressive nomination, received about fifteen
hundred votes and thus failed to qualify. Amlie received a
greater percentage of votes than Democrats normally receive
in the First District, and the Progressive percentage of the
primary vote declined, indicating that many Progressives had
entered the Democratic primary to vote for him.[9]

Now the La Follettes faced a dilemma. Their man did not
qualify in the primary and he did not file as an independent
candidate; Greenquist said that he did not "want anything to
obscure the paramount issue in this campaign."[10] What was
the paramount issue? The choice lay between Amlie and the
Republican nominee Lawrence Smith, who was simply against
anything Rooseveltian. The La Follettes favored Amlie's position on domestic matters, but they favored Smith's stand on
foreign affairs. Presumably their support for one or the other
would indicate what to them was "the paramount issue." Phil
La Follette related later that he and his brother were in a situation comparable to that which their father faced in 1912:[11]
there was so much wrong with each candidate that neither of
them deserved a La Follette vote. In 1912 the elder La Follette simply handed in a blank Presidential ballot; in 1941 Bob
and Phil La Follette were spared the necessity of making or
declining to make a formal choice, for they did not vote in the
First District. The La Follettes said nothing publicly after the
primary. Amlie felt that they preferred a Smith victory.[12] He
was probably right. At the special election on August 29,
Smith defeated Amlie by a two to one margin.

The special election brought the foreign policy split to
the surface and, in doing so, probably aggravated it. At the
November, 1941, convention of Young Progressives, Otto
Christenson, the Progressive nominee for Attorney General in
1940 and a supporter of President Roosevelt's policy, told the
delegates:

> Our attitude on foreign policy is a personal mat-
> ter with each of us. It is not a matter that should
> be permitted to disturb the solidarity of our party and
> the principles for which it stands.[13]

For the Progressive party, then, the handiest solution to the foreign policy issue was simply to ignore it. This the party did officially. The Progressives hoped that their solidarity on domestic matters would see them through the turbulent seas of international conflict. Yet, in 1941, the issue of foreign policy, no matter how inconvenient it was, simply could not be ignored.

Senator La Follette saw a deadly parallel between the present period and the course that the United States had followed prior to America's entry into World War I. "I feel as though I had walked into a movie only to discover that I had seen the picture years ago, under a somewhat different name and with a different cast."[14] He remembered that in 1917, America had not been directly attacked, that there had been no unanimity of opinion on the wisdom or the desirability of entering the conflict. His father had been one of the six Senators to vote against the declaration of war. In 1941 Senator La Follette probably feared that Roosevelt would climax his "aid-short-of-war" policies with the request that Congress declare war on Germany, a war in which the United States had no immediate interest.

The Japanese attack on Pearl Harbor took the decision out of America's hands. The United States had not willfully entered the war, as the La Follettes feared she would; rather, another nation had forced her hand. "This is not the time for talk, nor for dispute as to who's to blame," Phil La Follette said a few days after Pearl Harbor, as he prepared to enter the Army. "We have a man-sized job on our hands. Our country needs every American at the job where he can render the best service for America."[15] Senator La Follette and other non-interventionists gave whole-hearted support to the prosecution of the war. Pearl Harbor ended for the time being the debate over foreign policy. But what role should America play in world affairs? —this question of the basic nature of American foreign policy had divided Roosevelt and the La Follettes, but this difference of opinion now became submerged in the far more important problem of winning the war. The immediacy of the war and the desperate military situation which faced the Allies in the early months of 1942 obscured this fundamental schism; nothing, however, could eradicate it.

By 1944 the issue of American foreign policy would arise again.

The foreign policy issue had split the Progressive party. It also had complicated efforts that were made to unite the Progressives with either the Democrats or the Republicans in the period prior to the 1942 elections. In general, the Democrats wanted the Progressives to unite with them, while the Republicans feared that the Progressives would abandon their own sinking ship and return to the Grand Old Party. Whatever sentiment there was within the Progressive ranks for deserting their party generally favored a return to the Republicans; after all, Progressives hastened to point out, it was the Republican party from which they had sprung in 1934. They might have added that the cause of Republicanism in Wisconsin seemed brighter than at any time in more than a decade. Immediately after the 1940 election many Democrats and Progressives expressed concern that a split in liberal ranks had allowed the Republicans to capture the state-wide offices with less than a majority vote. As a result, they discussed a possible fusion of the liberal forces in Wisconsin. Two weeks after the 1940 election a group of Democratic liberals met in Milwaukee. With the blessing of state chairman Thomas R. King and national committeeman Charles E. Broughton, this group appointed a committee to negotiate a possible merger with the Progressives. Throughout 1941 and early 1942 many county Democratic organizations publicly invited the Progressives to join with them. In June, 1942, the Democratic state convention passed the following resolution urging the Progressives to abandon their party and come home to the party of Roosevelt:

> Whereas, we recognize that some of the most outstanding liberals in the United States and some of the most loyal are in the ranks of Wisconsin Progressives, now therefore be it resolved that we invite all liberals of the state of Wisconsin to unite for the purposes of national unity for the duration of the national emergency using the agency of the Democratic party on the basis that we pledge to support only such candidates as are loyal to the president and his program.[16]

In their invitations to the Progressives, the Democrats

stressed ideological arguments: the Progressives were united
in their support of Roosevelt's domestic program, so they should
join the Democrats to make their support more effective. "The
third parties of Minnesota and Wisconsin are now defeating
the purposes for which they were started," Tom Amlie pointed
out. "They were started to break the system of one political
party with two political heads." The situation has changed
now, for "fully 90 per cent of the nation's liberals have gone
into the president's party in order to more effectively support
him."[17] For the Democrats there were also more practical con-
siderations. In 1938 they had fallen into third place in three-
party Wisconsin. In 1940 they had solidified their grip on
last place. With the elimination of the Progressive party, the
worst fate that could befall Wisconsin Democrats would be to
rise to second place in a two-party state. In 1940 the Democrats and Progressives together obtained a majority of the
vote; state Democrats hoped that the combined vote would
bring them victory were the two parties united under the Democratic banner. Well-known Progressives, such as Orland S.
Loomis and Harold E. Stafford, and certainly Robert M. La Follette, Jr., could add considerable strength to the Democratic
ticket. Finally, the Progressives had drawn perhaps the greater
share of Wisconsin patronage from the Roosevelt administration in the 1930's; with the death of the Progressives, there
would be no one to get New Deal patronage except Democrats.

In these efforts, state Democrats were not ignored by the
national party and the Roosevelt administration. Leo T. Crowley, chairman of the Federal Deposit Insurance Corporation,
was Wisconsin's most prominent Democrat in national affairs.
After 1938, and during the war, Crowley was the chief dis-
penser of federal patronage in Wisconsin.[18] He was the
spokesman for the Roosevelt administration to Wisconsin
Democrats. Crowley made it clear that he would like to see
the Wisconsin Democrats and Progressives join forces—
though, of course, under the Democratic label. The attempts
to unite the two parties before the 1942 election failed because neither party was willing to give up its identity. The
war in Europe, and America's entry into the conflict, complicated these attempts, for the war made domestic politics far
less urgent and far less important; the United States was in

a war for survival.

The Progressives, in general, charged that the Wisconsin Democrats were hopelessly reactionary. William T. Evjue recognized this but he could not get over the fact that Franklin D. Roosevelt, the great progressive leader, was a Democrat. Evjue simply urged the Progressives to enter the Democratic party and take it over. "If the Progressive forces of this state so decide," Evjue declared, "they can easily capture the Democratic party in Wisconsin in 1944."[19] Most Progressives who considered leaving their party, however, favored joining the Republicans. The Democratic party just did not offer the future success that the Republican party could provide. The backbone of Progressive strength was the rural Scandinavian vote, which was traditionally Republican. Even if Progressive leaders were to go over to the Democratic party, tradition rather than ideology probably would prevail with the mass of Progressive voters, and they would simply return to the Republican party. Wisconsin's tradition of Republicanism was exerting a powerful influence upon Progressive politicians, an influence which would increase in strength until 1946. In early 1942, Paul Alfonsi, former Progressive Speaker of the State Assembly and a candidate for the 1940 Progressive nomination for Governor, entered the Republican primary for Tenth District Congressman and he urged other Progressives to follow him into the Republican party.[20] As the election year 1942 approached, the strongest force pulling the Progressives away from their party was pulling them toward the Republicans.

The Republican organization in Wisconsin viewed the prospect of a Progressive invasion with undisguised horror. The state chairman, Dr. C. L. Kolb, wanted the Republican state convention to endorse candidates that the party would support in the primary. By this device the Republicans could muster their resources behind their own candidates and thus prevent Progressives from winning Republican nominations. "Among many other important reasons," Kolb explained, "such an endorsement is an urgent necessity to prevent political opportunists from the two nearly decadent opposition parties from entering our ranks in the primary."[21] Thomas E. Coleman, an influential Madison Republican, also supported convention endorsement of candidates, and for precisely the same reason.

If the defeat in 1940 and the drift away from their party and the war were not enough, other problems beset the Progressives. In 1936, 1938, and 1940 the Socialists had not appeared on the Wisconsin ballot, for they had supported the Progressives. In the summer of 1941 the Socialists decided to leave the Progressives and put the Socialist column back on the ballot for the 1942 election. This action weakened the Progressive party still further.

With many Democrats urging the Progressives to join them, with many Progressives threatening to re-enter the Republican party, and with the Socialists leaving the Progressives, uncertainty surrounded the future course of the party as the election year 1942 opened. So far the most prominent Progressive had remained inactive in party affairs. Since his re-election Bob La Follette had ignored Wisconsin politics except for his support of Kenneth Greenquist in the special primary in 1941. He had kept silent when queried about possible fusion with either national party. Senator La Follette found himself leader of the Progressive party, a role that he did not want, a role that had been thrust upon him by his brother's defeat in 1938 and made more secure when Phil entered the Army in 1941 and went off to the South Pacific a few months later. In March, 1942, Bob wrote to his brother, saying that he expected merely

> to fight a rear guard action against reactionary measures even though it is unpopular and may lick me in 1946. Being in this mood my present feeling is that if our fellows jump into the Republican or Democratic parties I shall just stay out of the 1942 campaign. I am not in the mood to try and persuade anyone against his judgement to follow any particular course at this time. . . . Life is too short and the future too obscure to put me in any frame of mind where I want to tell others what to do. I shall take whatever satisfaction can be extracted from hell on earth by trying to do what seems right for myself.[22]

Bob was hardly spoiling for a vigorous fight to keep the Progressive party alive, nor was he happy that leadership of the party had been placed in his hands. For that reason he may have resented his brother's leaving Wisconsin and Progressive politics behind.[23] Under normal circumstances Bob would not willingly play the role of a party leader; with the war and the resulting year-around sessions of Congress, Bob desired the role of party leader even less.   Yet, by dint of his name and his position, his words and his actions would determine the course that the Progressives would follow.   Because he disliked this role, his words and actions were as few as possible.

In Wisconsin, for Democrats who wanted the Progressives to join with them and for Progressives who wanted to return to the Republican party, Orland Loomis emerged as a central figure.   He had made a strong race for Governor in 1940, and many believed that he would run again in 1942.   This made him, next to Senator La Follette, the most important man in the Progressive party. The only real question was what ticket Loomis would choose.   Immediately after the 1940 election Loomis listened attentively to Democratic overtures for a coalition of the liberal forces in Wisconsin.   "Apparently they [some Democrats] are now sincere about doing something for 1942," Loomis wrote. "The problem probably will be that they expect us to go into the Democratic party."[24]   Therein lay the problem: Progressives who wanted coalition wanted it under the Progressive label, while the Democrats wanted coalition under the Democratic banner. Democratic state chairman King tried to persuade Loomis to run for Governor as a Democrat in 1942. Loomis's campaign manager, Maurice B. Pasch, has insisted that Loomis never considered running for anything as a Democrat.[25]   In May, 1941, Loomis wrote to a friend, in not his most sterling prose, that: "Some fellows seem to do some worrying about some fellows leaving our group for other parties but I am not so very much concerned about that."[26]   In July, 1941, Loomis publicly denied that he would run as a Democrat, and added: "The Progressive ticket is my ticket. Whatever the Progressive party does, I shall be with it.   And the Progressive state central committee said very definitely that it was not interested in coalition with any other party.   That is my stand."[27] The implication seems to be that Loomis might run in the Republican party if the Progressives decided to reenter it. Indeed, some suspected that Loomis wanted the Progressives to do just that.

In early 1942, in the midst of these doubts that the Progressive party would continue its separate existence, Senator La Follette met with Orland Loomis in Washington. La Follette wanted to make sure that Loomis, if he ran for Governor, would run on the Progressive ticket, and not yield to the pressure of Democrats to run as a Democrat, or the temptation that Loomis probably felt to run as a Republican.[28] In April, 1942, La Follette called a Progressive leadership conference to meet in Madison. His desire to keep the Progressive party alive was widely reported in the press.[29] At this meeting La Follette asked that all Progressives "close ranks and stand shoulder to shoulder in the fight for Progressive principles under the Progressive banner." Then, in glowing tribute to the Progressive war-cries of old, he continued:

> Both of the old parties are shot through with Toryism. The war has only served to bring out their reactionary forces in greater strength than ever before. They are chained to a philosophy of government which is as archaic on the home front as are muskets and sailing ships on the war front. True, there are men of courage and vision in each of the old parties, but the tragic truth is they are compelled more and more to fight a rearguard action against the powerful reactionary forces in their parties.
>
> We can restore good government in Wisconsin if we close ranks now, if we roll up our sleeves and begin now a campaign of education which will bring the facts and the issues before the people of Wisconsin. I am supremely confident that if all the facts are made available to the electorate, the result in November will be a triumph for Progressive principles.

Senator La Follette pledged that he would "give every possible moment, in so far as the sessions of congress permit, to contacting the people of Wisconsin and to advancing the Progressive cause in the state." He laid the emphasis on Progressive principles and the Progressive movement, not the Progressive party. This was almost heresy for a party leader, who must try to instill the faithful with the conviction that their party is virtue incarnate. La Follette's statement could have been stronger, yet it was sufficiently clear. The 150 leaders, some of them quite reluctantly, voted unanimously to stay with the Progressive party for the 1942 campaign.[30]

Senator La Follette would not have had so much party leadership thrust upon him if someone in Wisconsin had been able to assert and provide the necessary direction. The party, in this respect, suffered for its close association with the La Follettes; it seemed that as long as a La Follette were active in public life no one else could properly assert authority. Orland Loomis, the only man in Wisconsin who conceivably could have taken some of the leadership burden from La Follette's shoulders, was a relatively colorless and unimaginative man, without force of personality. He seldom offended anyone. After the Madison conference, Robert H. North, secretary to Progressive Congressman Gehrmann, told Loomis that he regretted "very much" that Loomis, at the Madison meeting, had not positively taken the reigns of Progressive party leadership. "You realize, of course, that inasmuch as no one had actually assumed the leadership in Wisconsin that everything has to go through Bob's office."[31]

In June Loomis announced that he would run for Governor— as a Progressive. Democratic state chairman King became particularly bitter, claiming that Loomis had promised several times to run for Governor as a Democrat, but that he finally filed as a Progressive largely under pressure from Senator La Follette. "I spent the year 1941 trying to convince the Democrats of the state that we should unite all the liberals for the campaign of 1942," King recalled, "and to prove to our liberal friends we were sincere, we offered to accept Loomis as our candidate for governorship in 1942 on the Democratic ticket. On numerous occasions Loomis stated his acceptance of this plan, and only six weeks ago he still was agreeable. Last week he still wanted to talk it over but then Loomis filed his nomination papers for a Progressive candidacy."[32] Later in June the Progressives held another conference, this time at Stevens Point. In a speech to the gathering Senator La Follette charged that both the Democratic and Republican parties were hopelessly reactionary, and added, with perhaps a glance in Loomis's direction:

It is an inspiration to be with men and women who
have resisted the subtle and the sometimes not so
subtle pressures of the political Pied Pipers who
would lure us away from Progressive principles with
glib promises of easy victories and political patronage.

We can win and we shall win in this 1942 campaign, but only if all of us take off our coats, roll up
our sleeves, and yes, open our pocketbooks, in order
to give the reactionaries in both old parties the fight
of their lives.[33]

La Follette's word alone was probably enough to assure
that the Progressive party would stay alive for the fall campaign.   Aside from these two meetings, La Follette did little
else for the party until the last week of the fall campaign. In
a letter to Loomis he said, "Since the Madison conference, I
have written most of those who were invited and urged upon
them the importance of getting local tickets lined up at once."[34]
He probably expressed the same sentiment to other Progressives, but that hardly got the local tickets lined up.   Yet La
Follette had made the important decision that the Progressive
party should not be abandoned.   Bob La Follette considered
most problems with a manner both thorough and judicious. He
examined his ground with great care before he took a step.
Because he contemplated every move with such judiciousness
and with such care, he seldom moved very far very fast. Progressive principles had been imposed upon his conservative
temperament.   In matters of political action and organization
his actions revealed his caution, his conservatism.   In 1934
he had opposed the new departure in Wisconsin—it represented change which he felt was too sudden, too dramatic,
change which was fraught with peril.   Now, in 1942, to abandon the Progressive party would alter the political situation
in Wisconsin too suddenly, it would be a change fraught with
Peril. La Follette wanted to avoid making any decision on the
future of the party; if a decision had to be made, then he would
prefer the least taxing, the easiest one possible. The political activity in Wisconsin throughout 1941 and into early 1942
forced him to do something.   It was easier to decide to keep

the Progressive party alive than to make the far more difficult decision to abandon it altogether and to take all the steps necessary to find a political home elsewhere.

There were other reasons for La Follette's desire to keep the Progressive party alive. In his eight years as a Progressive Senator, he had discovered that being a member of an independent party had great advantages. It was a position of freedom and independence which he wanted to maintain.[35] Nineteen forty-six was a long way off, especially when a war situation accelerates the pace of events. In 1946 he might want to run for re-election as a Progressive, or he might want to run on another ticket. He neither wanted nor needed to make a decision on this question for a number of years. He did want to keep the Progressive party alive as an alternative for himself in 1946. To abandon the party now would destroy that alternative. Many Wisconsin Progressives, in particular Glenn D. Roberts, Progressive state chairman from 1942 to 1946, encouraged La Follette in this direction.[36] Finally Bob, as usual, did not want to do anything politically disagreeable to his brother. Mrs. Philip La Follette has said that Bob felt it his duty to Phil to try to keep the Progressive party alive.[37] On top of all this, war problems kept Senator La Follette in Washington, away from state issues and state politics. He was making it abundantly clear that he was more a Washington Senator than a Wisconsin Senator. About the organization or the problems of the Progressive party of Wisconsin he cared very little, except to insure that the party not die.

In the fall of 1942 the United States had its first Congressional campaign conducted under the pale of global war; the election was subdued and listless, almost a footnote to the news from Guadalcanal. In Wisconsin there was an added reason for a dull campaign, for it seemed so fully a Republican year. Apparently no one became excited about the imminent disaster which Progressives and Democrats almost promised the voters if the Republicans won. Loomis tried to run his campaign for Governor as independent of the La Follettes as possible. "The Progressive party of Wisconsin is not the party of any one man. It belongs to the men and women of Wisconsin," Loomis declared. "No one man at any time can claim the inalienable right to say that the Progressive party of Wisconsin belongs to him."[38]

The activity of the La Follettes was less than in any election year since Young Bob first entered the Senate. In the week before the election Senator La Follette made a brief tour of the state and spoke on behalf of the entire Progressive ticket. He campaigned as a partisan, playing his role as leader of the Progressive party, attacking the "broken promises . . . incredible maladministration, and record-breaking taxes" of the Heil administration.[39]   La Follette, as usual, probably found this task uncomfortable, if not downright distasteful; he was unhappy with his week of campaigning.   So, too, was Loomis.

Orland Loomis believed that only the unpopularity of Heil could elect him Governor.   Julius P. Heil was at some times profane, at most times colorful. He had gained a well-deserved reputation as a political buffoon, so much so that he was a very vulnerable target for political attack.[40]   Many state Republican leaders feared that Heil would jeopardize a Republican victory. He had run far behind other Republicans in 1940, defeating Loomis by less than 13,000 votes.   In 1942 Loomis pointed to the Heil administration with the alarm and indignation of a non-partisan public servant, and eschewed any role of Progressive party leadership. "The amazing feature of this campaign to me," Loomis said, "is that I have become a non-partisan candidate entirely through the voluntary action of the people. Republicans and Democrats have joined my following everywhere without attempting to cover up their switch to me."[41] The maladministration of Governor Heil and the need for unity behind the war effort have made this "a non-partisan election. . . . Republicans, Democrats and citizens of other political faiths, as well as the members of my own party, are back of my candidacy."[42] The man heading the Progressive ticket asserted that in the present campaign "party names and labels play a very insignificant part."[43]   The relationship between Orland Loomis and Senator La Follette was cordial but not entirely harmonious.   Soon after the 1940 election, Loomis had written with some bitterness that a few Progressives "have finally come to the conclusion that there are some other names that can get some votes besides the name of La Follette."[44] Loomis probably resented La Follette's activity in the 1942 campaign, for this undercut his independence of action and the non-partisan stance he deemed essential to his own victory.

The Wisconsin Democrats were, as two years before, harmless. They stood in no danger of winning, and their campaign attracted all the attention of a minor party. A few days before the election Leo T. Crowley endorsed Loomis, which implied administration support for the Progressives. Senate Majority Leader Alben W. Barkley of Kentucky, one of Bob's close friends in Washington, delivered a speech in Wisconsin in which he ignored any mention of the Democratic gubernatorial nominee, W. C. Sullivan.

When the results of the November 3 election were in, Progressives had suffered another setback. They lost ten of their twenty-nine seats in the state Legislature, and one of their three places in the House of Representatives. Progressive candidates for Lieutenant Governor, Secretary of State, State Treasurer and Attorney General were swamped by their Republican opponents, with margins ranging from 92,000 to 235,000 votes. As in 1940 Democrats ran a poor third in all state-wide races. Yet in the most important contest Orland Loomis defeated Governor Heil, 397,664 to 291,945 votes.[45] It was hardly a Progressive victory or even a Loomis victory. *The Wisconsin State Journal* said editorially that the "election was not a victory for Orland Loomis. It was a vote of protest AGAINST Julius Heil."[46] In the days after the election, Loomis continued his non-partisan posture: "I appeal to Wisconsin," the Governor-elect said, "to be united in a non-partisan way as never before to meet the problems of the day."[47] Despite Loomis's words, and despite their defeats in other races, Progressives attempted to regard his victory as a triumph for their party. Perhaps, many of them believed, the Progressive party could now be rebuilt to a position of dominance within the state and, after the war, the party could expand throughout the nation. The dream of 1934 could still come true.

"I think the happiest time in a candidate's life," Governor-elect Loomis said, "is after he is elected and before he takes office."[48] In the weeks after the election Loomis accepted overtures from Republicans for a harmonious session of the 1943 Legislature. On December 4, 1942, during the state budget hearings, the Governor-elect was taken to the hospital with a "cold." Within the next four days he suffered five heart attacks; in the early evening of December 7, 1942, Loomis died.

Never before in the history of Wisconsin had a Governor-elect died before he could take office. There was considerable doubt as to who would become Governor, or even how this was to be determined. The Progressive organization wanted a special election to settle the issue. In late December the state Supreme Court decided that the Republican Lieutenant Governor, eighty-year old Walter S. Goodland, should become the Acting Governor. On January 4, 1943, when Loomis would have been inaugurated, Goodland took the oath of office. This had been the only state-wide office won by the Progressives. Now it, too, belonged to the Republicans.

Governor Orland Loomis could have become the Progressive political leader in Wisconsin. If he had lived, his actions would have had a decisive impact upon the Progressive party. Loomis doubtless had considered running for re-election in 1944 as a Republican. Many have expressed the conviction that Loomis planned definitely to do just that.[49] His non-partisan campaign was essential to victory in 1942; it was also highly useful in preparation for 1944, facilitating his drift into the Republican party even before then. Yet Loomis was not a forceful person; whether he would have tried to take all the Progressives with him into the Republican party, and whether he could have done this successfully, is impossible to determine.

Loomis's death removed the only man who could have relieved Senator La Follette of some of the burden of Progressive party leadership. After Loomis's death, the future destiny of the party lay ever more clearly in La Follette's reluctant hands. Because he did not provide effective leadership Senator La Follette helped to seal his party's doom. After 1942 La Follette almost totally neglected political affairs in Wisconsin. His visits to the state became less frequent than before and often of limited success. He was, as always, in Washington, but the war, and not Washington, dominated the news. During the 1930's, when the nation's primary concern was the Great Depression, he was often in the headlines. During the war Senator La Follette faded out of public view and was less in the news than ever before in his career.

Defeat in 1942, the death of Loomis, and the war combined to subdue the Progressive party. The New Deal's domestic program had withdrawn much popular support from the Progressives. The war withdrew the popular enthusiasm necessary
to the survival of a new, reform party, crusading on a platform
of domestic issues.   With no state-wide offices to its credit
the party lacked an effective podium. In the state Legislature
the Progressives had been reduced to relative impotence, with
only nineteen of the one hundred and thirty-three seats; during
the war minority legislative action was far less effective as
a political tool than usual.   The Progressives realized that
they could not afford to lose any more strength. If they could
hold the line against further loss during the war, then after
the war perhaps the Progressive party could consolidate and
expand its strength.   The Progressive party had been built on
a program of domestic reform, and on domestic matters the
party displayed considerable unity.   When the European war
forced to the surface the issue of American foreign policy and
the question of America's role in the world, this unity was
shattered.   The party could survive only if during the war it
could prevent a further decline in its strength and if, after the
war, when the nation would pay far less attention to foreign
problems, its domestic program were again to arouse the enthusiasm it did in the mid-1930's.   Surely domestic matters
would again become the primary national concern with the
almost inevitable post-war depression, a depression Progressives predicted with gloom, a depression they felt necessary
to their own future. Yet, the Progressives first had to survive
the war.

Throughout 1943 and 1944 Senator La Follette expressed
his desire that the Progressive party be kept alive. "Genuine
political realignment," he said, will come after the war if the
question of whether "all the people" or "the few" are to benefit from modern science is to be decided through "political
action."   The forces pulsating in the 1930's for a third party
had been frozen by the war.   Yet realignment will come, after
the war, because progressive leadership of the Democratic
party is now "engulfed. . . as it allows big business to take
over the war effort."[50] "I personally favor the party continuing
its existence," La Follette said in the summer of 1943, "and

I hope it will have a full ticket in the field in 1944 for state, legislative, congressional offices and the U.S. senate." If the Progressives decided to join another party, La Follette indicated that he would abide by such a decision. "Naturally I believe in democratic procedure (spell that with a small D) and naturally would abide by any decision rendered by any representative cross-section of the rank and file party sentiment." He expressed no preference between joining either the Democrats or the Republicans——"That's a bridge we can only cross when we get to it and I hope we never get there." La Follette did not contemplate crossing that bridge in 1944. "The time has come to stop debating and get ready for the next campaign. The party is on the ballot and it's obviously pretty certain there will be a Progressive slate in the field in 1944."[51]

These were, however, simply public statements. The only help La Follette gave to the party was to voice support for it. The party organization itself was inert. There was no outstanding Progressive leader in Wisconsin. "The party, fruitlessly milling around without leadership except during the heat of a campaign," Aldric Revell observed in the spring of 1943, "is rapidly disintegrating for lack of energy, initiative, and incentive."[52]

Phil La Follette, still in the South Pacific, and Alfred Rogers, a longtime family friend, both suggested to Bob that he was spending too much time in Washington and, as a result, was losing contact with his constituents in Wisconsin. Phil pointed out that "Old Bob" had never let Washington duties prevent him from tending to his political fences in Wisconsin. Young Bob recognized this, but said that he had to stay in Washington most of the time because "never as much as now people are looking to Congress to help straighten out the mess created by the war and made worse by maladministration."[53]

On August 14, 1943, an "informal" meeting of Progressive leaders convened in Madison. Senator La Follette attended the meeting, the first time that he had met with party leaders since the Stevens Point conference of June, 1942. About fifty Progressive leaders, under La Follette's watchful eye, made the "emphatic" decision to have a full slate of Progressive candidates for the 1944 campaign.[54]

In May, 1944, a Progressive party convention met in Milwaukee, the first since the Fond du Lac Convention in 1934. By this time the sense of pessimism about the war which had prevailed in 1942 had disappeared almost entirely. Now that the tide of the war had turned, and the Allies were on the offensive, the post-war settlement was increasingly a subject of public discussion. There was no disagreement on the necessity of victory. But the question of the peace settlement and the foreign policy to pursue after victory had been won would provoke the same sort of split as between the "isolationists" and "interventionists" before the war.

The Progressive party convention demonstrated this very well. In a major speech, Senator La Follette attacked both the Democrats and the Republicans, and pointed with pride to the Progressives as the only haven of righteousness in a politically reactionary world. "The Progressives can be thankful that they have maintained their independence," La Follette said. His most important words, however, dealt with foreign affairs:

> Progressives are opposed to all efforts to commit the United States to a specific future course in world relationships so long as the people of the United States are still in the dark as to the peace demands and post-war objectives of the other United Nations, including Great Britain, China, and Russia.
>
> Progressives believe the United States should not take over a lease or rent a room in any international house until we know who is building that house, just how it is built, what the foundations are, and, most of all, whether the structure is to be a haven of hope for the common man of all countries or merely a super stockade to protect a ruthless imperialistic status quo.[55]

La Follette's words demonstrated his caution, his reluctance to rush into any new venture, and little enthusiasm for the international commitments President Roosevelt was making for the United States. Senator La Follette made it clear that he was far less willing than the President for the United States to play an active role in world affairs. Shortly after Roosevelt's death La Follette told how these differences had affected his relationship with the President: "Naturally, the sharp, fundamental disagreement over foreign policy lessened our contacts, and with the entry of this country into the war and the terrific additional burdens it entailed upon the president, I saw him infrequently during the last few years."[56] The "sharp, fundamental disagreement over foreign policy" persisted. By a vote of 666 to two, the Progressive Convention supported Senator La Follette's position.

La Follette may have been motivated to deliver his speech, at least in part, by the April 4 Wisconsin Presidential primary. Wendell Willkie had campaigned vigorously in the state, standing on a platform of support for Roosevelt's foreign policy, of broad international co-operation, of "One-Worldism." The isolationist forces determined to defeat Willkie in the Wisconsin primary. After an extensive and an exhaustive campaign, Willkie was soundly defeated by the forces of New York Governor Thomas E. Dewey, who had not raised a finger in his own behalf. If the primary was a contest between the internationalists and the isolationists, as it appeared to be, then the isolationists clearly won. The foreign policy which La Follette supported in May had been endorsed by Wisconsin in April.

Senator La Follette asked that the Progressive party be kept alive, and it was kept alive. The primary results in August, 1944, however, gave the Progressives little reason for optimism. Their nominees for Governor and Senator, Alexander Benz and Harry Sauthoff, and their candidates for Lieutenant Governor and Attorney General, qualified for a place on the general election ballot, but by the slenderest of margins. Their candidate for Secretary of State failed to qualify. Furthermore, though thirty Progressives qualified for state legislative races, twenty-three additional Progressive candidates in other legislative districts did not qualify.[57] If all their candidates to the state Legislature were to be elected, they would still fall far short of a majority. The Progressive party, for the first time in its life, had run a distant third in the primary.

The Republicans had the huge moneybags and the contests on the county level to attract a sizeable primary vote, Senator La Follette told the party faithful. The reactionaries are mistaken if they believe that "the Progressive party or the principles it stands for" had been "knocked out of the political life of Wisconsin." Besides, the party had performed poorly in the primaries of 1940 and 1942 only to come back strong in the general election. In other words, the Progressives were merely running true to form. La Follette added that he was "ready, willing, and anxious" to put on an "aggressive campaign" for his party.[58] The Progressives still had visions of bouncing back after the war. "The Progressive party hierarchy hopes to hold the party together until after the war when Col. Philip La Follette returns from the South Pacific," Aldric Revell wrote in the fall. "It is their belief that the party could sweep to power again during the post-war depression days."[59]

The Progressive platform committee, meeting later in August, had to consider two divisive issues. One was foreign policy; the other was a fourth term for President Roosevelt. La Follette, disenchanted with the Roosevelt administration at home and abroad, was reluctant to support the President. Progressives Leo Vaudreuil, a candidate for the 1944 gubernatorial nomination, former chairman Jack K. Kyle, and Assemblyman Earl Mullen wanted the party to support Roosevelt's foreign policy and his quest for a fourth term. The committee reached a compromise: it modified the isolationist position of the May convention by adopting a more pro-Roosevelt position on international co-operation, yet, to please La Follette, the party did not officially endorse the President. Senator La Follette had supported Roosevelt in 1932, 1936, and 1940, but in 1944 he remained neutral. "But instead of speaking up," La Follette said, "Pres. Roosevelt and Gov. Dewey seem to have entered into a conspiracy of silence on the vital issues of American foreign policy. Once again, as in 1940, the people are to be deprived of any effective choice on the most important issues of this campaign."[60] In October a number of leading pro-Roosevelt Progressives formed a "Progressives for Roosevelt" committee. Yet, without La Follette's support for the President, the Roosevelt administration gave its full support to the state Democrats for the first time since the formation of the Progressive party.

Senator La Follette, as had become his custom, devoted only a few days before the election to campaigning. "The Progressive party can be proud of its candidates in this campaign," La Follette told his listeners. "No voter will have to be ashamed if he votes the Progressive ticket."[61] These were not the words to inspire mass enthusiasm for his party. "The Progressive party's 1944 platform," La Follette said, "is based on the three-fold objective of winning the war promptly, building an economy of abundance for America, and joining with other nations to write and enforce a just and democratic peace."[62] Never before had La Follette's campaigns been quite so inoffensive.

Before the election the Progressives received a jolt when their long-time newspaper ally, *The Capital Times*, endorsed the Democratic candidates for Governor and Senator. These two men, Daniel W. Hoan and Howard J. McMurray, were hardly the type of reactionary that Progressives charged had been leading the Wisconsin Democrats. Hoan, for twenty-four years Mayor of Milwaukee, had called himself a Socialist. McMurray, a professor of political science, was in 1944 the Congressman from Milwaukee's Fifth District. In Congress he was a Roosevelt supporter on both domestic and foreign affairs. With the support of many Wisconsin Progressives, and the full support of the national Democratic party, the state Democrats seemed in a stronger position than at any time since 1932, though few of them harbored any hopes for victory. The Republicans still regarded the Progressives as their main opponents. The election produced the expected Republican victory. They won all state-wide offices, and Senator Alexander Wiley was re-elected. Yet, the Democrats showed unexpected strength, finishing a strong second. Hoan received 536,357 votes, compared with Governor Goodland's 697,740. McMurray lost to Senator Wiley by 634,513 to 557,144 votes. For the first time of its life the Progressive party finished third, receiving but six per cent of the vote. Benz garnered only 76,028 votes for Governor, and Sauthoff received 73,089 votes in his race for the Senate.[63] The Progressives lost eight of their nineteen seats in the state Legislature, and retained but one seat in the House of Representatives. Most of the loss in the Progressive strength went to the Democrats, mainly in the industrial areas in Kenosha, Racine, and Milwaukee counties. Both in state and nation organized labor had allied itself firmly with the Democratic party.

The Progressive party had depended upon the appeal of its domestic issues for its unity and for its separate existence. The war had eclipsed these issues. Because foreign policy so seriously split the Progressives, their party could not retain its unity until foreign policy ceased to be the primary national concern, nor could it maintain its separate existence unless it again was able to base its strength on the issues of domestic economy and reform. To stay alive the party had to survive the war, and to survive the war the party had to prevent any further decline in its strength. This, clearly, it had not done.

Chapter V

THE DEATH OF THE PROGRESSIVE PARTY

The 1944 election left the Progressive party of Wisconsin demoralized, and the prospects for its future never appeared bleaker. The party faced the fact reluctantly. State chairman Glenn D. Roberts expressed confidence in the survival of progressive principles, not particularly encouraging words to the organization. Senator Robert M. La Follette's words, however, carried the most weight, for he remained the acknowledged leader of the party. A few days after the 1944 election, he said:

> The Progressive movement has been tested and tempered by a score of defeats in the past. The defeat Tuesday will make us, I feel certain, better and stauncher fighters in the great battles ahead, for regardless of anything else, the principles of the Progressive movement must yet be translated into the law of our state and land. Americans of all political beliefs have a war to win. Progressives have a crusade to win as well.[1]

Progressive principles and the Progressive movement would survive, but what about the Progressive party? On this point La Follette remained vague. Until March, 1946, he did not discuss publicly his political plans, nor did he give any indication of what course he thought the Progressive party should follow.

After the 1944 election it was widely assumed in Wisconsin

that the Progressive party would officially disband, and for two good reasons. First, most politicians and political observers believed that no one, not even a La Follette, could win on the Progressive ticket, and Senator La Follette was up for re-election in 1946. He was only fifty years old and few doubted that he would run. In 1942 and 1944 he had wanted to keep the Progressive party alive. He felt that it might serve a useful function as soon as the war was over; moreover, his own candidacy was not at stake, and he had wanted to keep the party alive as a possible alternative for himself in 1946. After the 1944 election, however, the Progressive party was so weak that it seemed capable of carrying no one, not even a La Follette, to victory.

A second factor which encouraged the belief that the Progressive party would disband was the coming end of the war. In late 1944 and early 1945 the Allies' triumph was no longer in doubt. With victory the intense activity of the war years would slacken and give way to "normalcy." The armed forces would return home, the economy would produce butter, not guns; dramatic change would be apparent in all phases of life. During the war the Progressives had insisted that the party's revival would have to wait until the war was over. Yet, its poor showing in 1944 had killed the party's chance for survival under any circumstances. Such an atmosphere of immediate and drastic change, such an obvious transition period as the end of World War II, would facilitate the disappearance of the Progressive party.

After 1938 an ever-increasing number of Progressives deserted their party. In some cases they joined the Democrats; in most cases, however, they returned to the Republican banner. In 1942 and 1944 only the words of Senator La Follette had prevented this drift to the Republican party from becoming an uncontrollable landslide. Aldric Revell noted, in the spring of 1943, that "by far the largest segment of the party feels that the Progressives could accomplish more, both for themselves and for the state, in returning to the Republican party and liberalizing that organization."[2] So devastating were the results of 1944 that now loud rumblings were heard of a wholesale desertion of the party.

The Progressive party had drawn much of its strength from

the rural areas in western Wisconsin; were the Progressive party to disband these supporters probably would revert to their old habit of voting Republican. In the industrial areas along Lake Michigan, particularly the counties of Kenosha, Racine, and Milwaukee, the Democrats were gaining strength, and they were gaining at the expense of the Progressives. After 1944, then, two major forces pulled at what remained of the Progressive party: one force, mainly Progressives from rural areas, wanted the party to disband and return to the Republicans; the other major force, mainly from the industrial areas, wanted the Progressives to join the party of Roosevelt. A faction within the party tried to resist both pressures and keep the Progressives alive for 1946 and beyond. The Socialists also got into the act: in November, 1945, their state executive committee extended a "cordial invitation" to the Progressives to join with them.[3] By early 1946, after the war was over, the major political question in Wisconsin was: Which way, Progressives?

The force pulling the Progressives toward the Republican party was undoubtedly the strongest. The La Follettes had operated as Republicans until 1934. More than that, in 1945 and 1946 Wisconsin seemed as safely a Republican state as it had been before the Great Depression. But the men who now controlled the Republican party—those who had been Stalwarts in the 1920's—wanted nothing to do with the Progressives. They looked upon a Progressive invasion of their party with undisguised horror.

On July 19, 1943, Thomas E. Coleman became state chairman of the Republican party. He possessed an antipathy for La Follette—any La Follette. Years later a long-time observer of Wisconsin politics wrote: "Many who have pondered Coleman's career believe he entered politics originally because of his compulsive desire to drive the La Follettes out of public life." Coleman seems "impelled to recall the time that he and other children built a winter slide on a Madison hill and the La Follette boys, Phil and Bob, who had not helped to make the slide, came along and used it. He caps this story off with the comment, 'They lived off some other person's work all their lives.'"[4] As he geared the Republican party for the 1946 campaign, Coleman saw the defeat of Senator La Follette as the *sine qua non* to success. One Progressive writer noted that many Republican leaders "would consider it a Republican victory if they could defeat Sen. La Follette and lose all other offices."[5] "More than anything else," a Republican reporter said, "they want to defeat Bob."[6] Coleman believed that the surest way to defeat La Follette in 1946 would be to force him to run as a Progressive. In a three-way race in the general election, Coleman felt that a Republican could most easily defeat La Follette. Moreover, were La Follette to run for the Republican Senate nomination and win it, Coleman's power and influence in the Wisconsin Republican party would evaporate.

Early in 1945 Coleman sponsored a bill in the state Legislature which provided that a candidate, or the "supporter" of a candidate in one party in 1944 could not be a candidate in another party in 1946. The primary objective of Coleman's bill was to prevent Senator La Follette from running in the Republican primary. "We do not intend to offer the Republican party organization as the vehicle for the election or re-election of members of other parties," Coleman said. "We will welcome Progressive voters but not Progressive candidates who are anti-Republican in their views. . . . I consider Sen. La Follette's principles to be anti-Republican."[7] When asked if the bill were aimed at the Progressives, Coleman replied: "That isn't the purpose of it. No other primary in the country has such a wide open status as ours. This will strengthen the primary."[8] Wisconsin Republicans generally supported the Coleman bill. Governor Goodland said originally that he would support it "if it didn't go too far."[9] In February, 1945, Coleman testified on the merits of his proposal: "This law will prevent a wholesale shifting of office-holders from one party to another whenever a single party may seem to have better than ordinary prospects. It will insure a better quality in candidates because they will be of their party and will have a responsibility to their party."[10]

In February a caucus of Democratic legislators went on record against the bill. They opposed it because it would keep La Follette and other Progressives from running as Democrats. The Democratic floor leader in the Assembly, Leland S. McParland, said: "The only thing you Republicans fear is that Young Bob will run on the Republican ticket, and if he does he'll beat you and you know it. We would welcome him in the Democratic party as we would welcome any man that is qualified to run."[11] Significantly, the Executive Board of the Wisconsin C.I.O. also opposed the bill because, among other things, it "attempts to freeze the situation of the three parties."[12]

There was enough Republican opposition in the state Legislature to the original bill that Coleman was forced to modify it. After a protracted battle a compromise bill, strongly supported by Coleman, went to Governor Walter S. Goodland in June, 1945. Goodland vetoed it. "This bill would prevent the party from choosing its candidates freely," the Governor said, "by setting up barriers as to requirements and time. This is unwarranted and indefensible in a democracy."[13] The Legislature could not muster the two-thirds vote to over-ride the Governor's veto. Progressives and Democrats were pleased, but chairman Coleman was outraged. "Gov. Goodland gave his word to me repeatedly that he would permit it to become law," the disconsolate chairman said.[14] The relationship between Coleman and Goodland already had been strained; the veto, it seemed, produced an irrevocable break between the two men.

The Governor's veto thwarted Coleman's attempt to legislate La Follette in the Progressive party for 1946. After June, 1945, therefore, Coleman directed his energies to defeating La Follette in the Republican primary. In the fall of 1945 the party chairman made a tour of the state, visiting the various county organizations. He told the faithful of the manifold sins of Glenn D. Roberts, William T. Evjue, and, above all, Robert M. La Follette, Jr.—Wisconsin must be disinfected of these elements. "If they [the Progressives] want to try the Republican primary, we will have the candidates and the organization and the voting support to defeat them. If those office seekers decide to desert their party in 1946 the plans we have made need not be changed, even though they decided to jump our way."[15] The lyrics were often modified, but the melody remained the same: "If a Progressive wants office, let him have courage enough and enough political honesty to fight it out in a general election with the label of the party he created in 1934. But, if he does not have that courage, meet him with a supported candidate that can beat him in the primary."[16] Then Coleman charged that the name long associated with the fight against special privilege was itself a beneficiary of special privilege. He attacked Roberts, Evjue, and La Follette for their financial interest in two radio stations—WIBA in Madison and WEMP in Milwaukee. "Until this week, the public had no knowledge of Sen. La Follette's commercial advantage from the use of such a [radio] license," Coleman boomed. "In view of his years of hammering away at special privileges, does he now contend that it is proper and ethical for him, a U.S. senator, to use any influence on a federal agency which permits him to make additional income far greater than his salary as U.S. senator? . . . This is special privilege obtained through political influence."[17] Coleman repeated this refrain throughout the fall of 1945.

Thomas E. Coleman's desire to defeat La Follette and the Progressives was felt by most state Republican leaders. Yet there were a few Wisconsin Republican leaders who flirted with heresy by publicly welcoming the Progressives into their party. The Milwaukee Republican organization declared that it would "welcome" the Progressives.[18] This action was taken under the influence of Lansing Hoyt, who had been active in America First before the United States entered the war. "I feel that if Sen. La Follette should choose to run on the Republican ticket he should be supported because of his record in congress. He would help every other candidate on the Republican ticket," Hoyt said.[19] In Milwaukee County the Democrats dominated politics; Milwaukee Republicans saw that La Follette at the head of their ticket would strengthen them. Besides, Hoyt added, Senator La Follette "is a good American who is not a left-wing Communist."[20] This conservative and strongly pro-American support may not have pleased La Follette. Within Wisconsin it was far less important than the words and actions of the state's leading Republican heretic, Walter S. Goodland.

Shortly after his victory in 1944 Governor Goodland invited the Progressives to join the Republican party.[21] Since he had become Acting Governor in 1943 Goodland had been frequently at odds with the Republican organization and the Republican controlled Legislature. He was often on good terms

with Progressive leaders and legislators and drew praise from
them.   Morris Rubin, editor of La Follette's paper *The Progressive*, said that "Walter Goodland is one of the finest gov-
ernors Wisconsin has ever had."[22] The Governor's veto of the
Coleman bill pleased the Progressives. It was widely regarded
as a prelude to a Goodland-La Follette alliance, whereby La
Follette would receive the support of the popular Governor
whether Goodland himself ran for re-election or not.   Harry
Sauthoff expressed the sentiment of many Progressives when
he said: "I think we ought to endorse Goodland and get back
into the Republican primary."[23] The Progressives, Miles Mc-
Millin wrote,

> may come out for Goodland and send him and La Fol-
> lette to the barrier in the fall campaign. Progressives
> could support Goodland without compunction, for he
> has stood by them—and they by him—on some of the
> most controversial issues to come before the legisla-
> ture.   The combination of Goodland and La Follette
> would cause the Old Guard a herd of nightmares.
> Goodland, despite his advanced age, is, they con-
> cede, unbeatable.[24]

Characteristically, La Follette made no moves to effect
an alliance. In the fall of 1945 Goodland sent a personal representative to Washington to talk with Major General Ralph
M. Immell, who had just returned from the European front. Immell was an old La Follette family friend, and he was closely
identified with the La Follettes and the Progressives. He had
been the public works administrator in Wisconsin in the 1930's,
and he had served as executive director of the National Progressives of America in 1938. Goodland's representative asked
Immell, as Immell recalls it, to consider running for Governor
in the Republican primary with the Governor's support.   Senator La Follette was not specifically discussed, yet if Immell
were to accept the support of the Governor, this would virtually
assure that La Follette would receive the same blessing. Two
or three months later Immell talked directly with Goodland
about his offer.   Immell says that he believed that the Governor had no intention to be a candidate for re-election.[25]
    On March 15, 1946, Governor Goodland quite unexpectedly

announced that he would run for re-election, and he reiterated his invitation to the Progressives: "I have said before that they ought to be back in the Republican party and I still think that's where they belong, but it is up to them."[26] The Governor also attacked the Republican Legislature, and, implicitly, Coleman's domination of the party. The rift in the Republican party widened still further. Significantly, the Governor's announcement came just two days before the Progressives were to meet at Portage to decide the future course of their party, and it was probably an open bid for Progressive support against the Coleman faction. To win Goodland's support, or just to keep him neutral, Progressives would have to do nothing to antagonize him. The Governor's announcement hardly pleased Ralph Immell; he reports being astounded by it.[27] Coleman responded with another stinging blast at La Follette and other Progressive leaders.

Wisconsin Democrats, as a whole, viewed a Progressive invasion of their party in a much different light—they welcomed it. By 1946 Democrats in Wisconsin had become habituated to being out of power. Senator La Follette was a proven vote-getter who might be able to carry them to power within the state. The most influential state Democrats tried to lure the Progressives their way. On several occasions state chairman Robert Tehan publicly invited the Progressives to join the Democratic party, and he talked with La Follette about it. In November, 1945, Tehan said that the state committee was "renewing its invitation asking all Progressives into the Democratic party."[28] The next day the party's state central committee passed the following resolution:

> The members of the Democratic state central committee in convention assembled do herewith most heartily invite into the Democratic party all citizens of this state of Wisconsin who subscribe with us to the liberal and forward looking principles, and particularly former members of the Progressive party.[29]

The Democrats wanted La Follette to be their candidate for Senator in 1946. They added a sharp edge to their invitation by making it clear that were Senator La Follette to run as a Republican or as a Progressive, they would strenuously op-

pose him.   Daniel W. Hoan and Howard J. McMurray tried to
persuade La Follette to join the Democratic party.   McMurray
has described his efforts:

> I visited with Senator La Follette early in 1946
> in an attempt to get him to become the Democratic
> candidate for the United States Senate.   Although I
> was not an officer in the Democratic party in Wis-
> consin, I promised Senator La Follette that he could
> have the Democratic nomination without any serious
> opposition whatsoever.   All he had to do was to join
> forces with us to eliminate the reactionary Republican
> regime which was in control of the government in Wis-
> consin.   I promised him that I would stay out of the
> race and that I would campaign for him, both in the
> primary and in the general election.

McMurray added that if La Follette ran as a Republican, he
would oppose him.[30] Until the Progressives met at Portage to
decide what to do with their party, these Democrats did not
cease in their efforts to lure La Follette and his following their
way.

A few days prior to the Portage Convention President Truman's Secretary of Commerce sent a letter to McMurray, expressing his hope that the Progressives march *en masse* into
the Democratic party: "The two-party system in America is
made inevitable in the long run by several factors in our constitution, our state laws and our customs. . . . should any third
party be able to corral the electoral vote of four or five states
the presidential election would probably be decided in the
house in a manner so undemocratic that the people would not
stand for it. . . . The Progressives of Wisconsin with their great
tradition of liberal action should come home to the party of
Roosevelt, rather than return to the party of Hoover," Henry A.
Wallace concluded, and "revert to the historic two-party system."[31]

The prevailing sentiment among Wisconsin Democrats to
encourage the Progressives to join with them was not unanimous.   Gustave J. Keller, in a letter to state chairman Tehan,
urged the party to be unmercifully blunt: "Bob La Follette, we
do not want you on the Democratic ticket. Your program is not

ours."[32]   In the summer of 1940 Keller had publicly invited
Senator La Follette into the Democratic party.   Charles E.
Broughton, former national committeeman, urged that La Follette not be invited to join the Democrats; he criticized La
Follette "for trying to ride into office as an admirer of President Roosevelt when he in turn was his most bitter political
enemy."[33]   Broughton, like Keller, had spoken from a different
platform in 1940 when he had urged La Follette's election over
the Democratic candidate, James E. Finnegan.   Just after La
Follette's 1940 victory, Broughton had said editorially that La
Follette "belongs" in the Democratic party.[34]   In 1946 Keller
and Broughton represented a small, minority view within their
party, as Governor Goodland did for the Republicans.   In the
main, as 1946 opened, Democrats did want the Progressives
every bit as much as the Republicans did not.

  Election year 1946 focused on Senator Robert M. La Follette, Jr.   He, more than any other individual, dominated the
planning of Wisconsin's three parties. The Progressives' major
objective was to re-elect La Follette, the Republicans' major
objective was to defeat La Follette, and the Democrats' major
objective was simply to elect anybody.   The war had kept La
Follette's name out of the news, and he had not played his role
as a state political leader.   "What's happened to Bob La Follette?" Bill Evjue asked in March, 1945.   "This is a question
being asked with increased frequency by Wisconsin Progressives and liberals who have been watching the deliberations of
the United States senate in recent months."[35]   In August, 1945, La
Follette granted a newspaper interview, but he made it clear
that he would make no "political decision or announcement"
regarding his candidacy or the party on which he would run
for "some time," and that, for the present, he would prefer
not to discuss it.[36]   On his infrequent trips to Wisconsin he
had not taken part in political activities.   On Saturday, November 10, 1945, a special Progressive committee to determine the future course of the party met in Madison.   Senator
La Follette was in Madison that day, but he did not attend the
meeting.   Instead he watched Northwestern defeat Wisconsin
28—14 at the Homecoming Game.

  In Washington Senator La Follette was preoccupied by
two major issues.   First, with the coming end of the war, he

was more openly expressing his views on world affairs. After many months of preparation he delivered a major foreign policy speech in the Senate on May 31, 1945. La Follette was apprehensive about the events of recent months, particularly in Eastern Europe, and he felt that the San Francisco conference to establish the United Nations had "been oversold to the American people. . . . Thus far we have been traveling a road which, almost step by step, parallels the tragic road we took after the First World War. Unless we change our direction soon, we shall find that our fantastic expenditure of men, money, and materials has brought us only a short and uneasy truce—not the enduring peace we pray for and seek."[37]

The second matter that preoccupied him was the reorganization of Congress. In March, 1945, he was appointed chairman of a joint Senate-House committee to study the matter. There is a "growing belief that Congress is not adequate to the 'needs of modern government,'" La Follette had written in 1943. "If the control of government policy is to remain with the people's elected representatives, as the framers of the Constitution intended it should, and not drift into the hands of a relatively irresponsible bureaucracy, Congress will have to streamline its organization."[38] The post-war settlement, Congressional reorganization, and other pressing matters in Washington, in addition to his natural distaste for political activity, kept Senator La Follette from exercising any effective control or leadership over the Progressive party.

In January, 1945, the Progressive party appointed a committee to determine how the party could best decide its future course. A year later, on the committee's recommendation, the party called a convention to meet on March 17 at Portage, Wisconsin. The only business of this convention would be to decide the future course of the party. Delegates were to be chosen by county on the basis of one delegate for every five hundred votes cast in the 1940 primary; each county was guaranteed a minimum of three delegates. There was little doubt throughout Wisconsin that the Progressives would decide to return *en masse* to the Republican party: the press spoke in terms of "when the Progressives return," not "if the Progressives return." The press had a glorious time with the upcoming Portage Convention; expediency and sheer opportunism would make a mockery of political principles. *The Wisconsin State Journal* commented that "Progressives — meaning Robert La Follette — are returning to the GOP as surely as it says so in the script written for the March 17 'convention' by the La Follettes, the same La Follettes who have tied the strings and will manipulate the puppets at Portage."[39] In May, 1934, there was little doubt that the Fond du Lac Convention would form a separate Progressive party. Now, in March, 1946, there was little doubt that the Portage Convention would dissolve that party.

On Sunday, March 17, 1946, just under five hundred delegates gathered in the armory at Portage. Noticeably absent from the list of delegates were Thomas R. Amlie, William T. Evjue, Philip F. La Follette, and Robert M. La Follette, Jr. — the four men most responsible for the formation of the Progressive party in 1934. Amlie, as we have seen, had become a Democrat, and he was attempting to urge the rest of the misguided flock to come home to the party of the Great White Progressive Father, now gone to his eternal rest. Evjue was still issuing written thunderbolts; on this Sunday he was in Madison writing an editorial berating the brothers La Follette for selling out principle to political expediency. Philip La Follette, the driving force behind the party during his years as Governor, rested in quiet seclusion at his home in Madison. His absence surprised many delegates; one friendly observer said that the most asked question at the convention was: "Where's Phil? Isn't he going to get here?"[40] Among other reasons, he may have stayed away from Portage so that there would be no danger that his presence would spark a spontaneous demonstration to keep the party alive. Robert M. La Follette, Jr. was at Portage, but he was not a delegate. Until this time he had declined to say anything publicly about his political future or the course he believed the Progressive party should follow. La Follette apparently "has not raised his eyebrows or winked by way of tipping off his political lieutenants," one reporter wrote, "so they are standing around in the shadows of mystery."[41] Now he still declined to give any interviews, and he still refused to say what he thought the party should do.

Publicly La Follette's silence had been complete. Privately, he had discussed the matter with a few friends and close political associates. During 1945 he had expressed the thought to at least two of his friends that he "might be happier" not to run for re-election.[42]   In recent years campaigning had become an especially unpleasant task for him. He was effective at it, but he disliked it. The prospect of a rough campaign in 1946 held out no appeal for him. Yet, since he had become his father's secretary at the age of twenty-four he had known no other line of work than the legislative branch of government, and he genuinely enjoyed serving in Congress. He wanted to remain a United States Senator.   He would prefer to be re-elected without any campaigning.   If he had to campaign at all, he would prefer to do as little as possible.   He was not in robust health, and the prospect of a long, hard, tough fight, with uncertain chances for victory, might have dissuaded him from running in 1946. Yet his supporters in Wisconsin assured him that his own position was strong, and that victory, especially on the Republican ticket, would not be difficult.   With this encouragement La Follette probably made his decision by early 1946 that the Progressives should return to the Republican party.[43]   As he rode on the train from Chicago to Portage on Saturday, March 16, he had with him a speech prepared with the help of his assistant, William R. Voigt, a speech which expressed La Follette's reasons for deciding to return to the Republican party.   Characteristically he was still brooding about the events which lay ahead at Portage; he still worried about the speech that he carried with him and whether the decision he had made was the correct one.[44] He was not looking forward to the weekend.

The mayor of Portage gave a brief welcoming address after the convention came to order at 10:00 A.M.   Then the only business of the convention was at hand.   "It was something like a New England town meeting," a *New York Times* correspondent said, "in which everyone who wished to talk was accorded exactly five minutes to express his views before the vote was taken."[45]   In rapid succession forty-three Progressives told the gathering why the Progressives should return to the Republicans, why they should join the Democrats, why they should maintain their party identity, why they should join the Socialists. One farmer rose and said, "If this is a funeral, it's a strange one, because we're having trouble getting the corpse into the grave."[46] The speeches were impassioned, disorderliness ruled on the floor, nerves were frayed, tempers flared. Howard J. McMurray was at the convention, fruitlessly trying to pull the Progressives into the Democratic party. During the proceedings he told Glenn Roberts, as Roberts has remembered it, "I won't get elected, but I'll see that Bob doesn't."[47] Of the forty-three speakers, eighteen spoke for the Republicans, fourteen for maintaining the Progressive party, nine for the Democrats, and one for the Socialists. Each speech produced intermittent boos and cheers; emotions remained at a fever-pitch throughout the day. Those speakers who favored joining the Republicans also, to the delight of the delegates, condemned Harding, Hoover, Landon, Dewey, and Robert Taft. The assembled Progressives denounced "Harding and his Ohio gang" with a vigor and vehemence matched only by their response to "Truman and his new Missouri gang." Only one name produced cheers alone—Franklin D. Roosevelt.[48]

Senator La Follette had been scheduled to speak after the delegates had voted and formally made their choice. He would have preferred to keep it this way to avoid both the appearance and the reality of dictation. The convention, however, had not gone entirely as planned. When, for example, state chairman Roberts discovered that the Grant County delegation was pledged to vote to keep the party alive, he was furious. "That's being much too sentimental," he exclaimed.[49] Sentiment for maintaining the Progressive party ran so strongly that Roberts and other Progressive leaders feared that this feeling might prevail; to prevent this they requested La Follette to speak before the voting began. La Follette did so only when this appeared necessary to assure that the convention would decide to take the Progressives into the Republican party. Many delegates would vote as he requested, even though they might perfer a course other than the one he indicated.

In 1940, 1942, and 1944 Senator La Follette had held together a disintegrating Progressive party by pleas that it not be abandoned. Now, in the early afternoon of March 17, Robert M. La Follette, Jr. again held the stage of decision. This time he realized that the situation for his party was hopeless. He began by outlining the achievements of his father—eulo-

gies of "Old Bob" were standard procedure at Progressive gath-
erings—yet, he pointed out, all that his father had accomplished was done while he remained within the Republican
party. The Progressive party was formed in 1934 in the hope
that it would develop on a national scale. Phil La Follette's
attempt to form a national party in 1938 had failed. In 1940
there was still hope that the party would yet develop on a national basis. Times, however, had changed. "The war, which
eclipsed all domestic and state issues, snuffed out the last
hope for a national Progressive party at this time." The Progressive party of Wisconsin, La Follette pointed out, had never
been fully organized on the local level; in 1944 there were
tickets in less than a dozen counties. The party was at the
end of the line. "Thus, fellow progressives, we are here to
recognize a situation, not to create one." If our own vehicle
has lost its power, where, then, can we turn? "True, we have
had no invitations from the self-appointed boss of the Wisconsin Republican party or from the Communist party. But
Progressives would be insulted if they received engraved invitations to join up with either Colemanism or communism."
As for the Democratic party, "it is now stalled on dead cen-
ter. . . . It is clear from the record that the Democratic party
is not our hope for a liberal instrument for political action.
. . . The Democratic party of this state is a machine-minded
organization without principle or program." Besides, it has
won only once in the last fifty years. As for the Republicans,
there is a rising "liberal movement within the party led by
Senators Aiken and Morse." Despite Coleman, whom the Progressives vowed to remove, and despite all of the other evils
manifest in Republicanism, "I am convinced that the Republican party of Wisconsin offers us the best opportunity for the
advancement of Progressive principles. Wisconsin has always been a Republican state—and by this I don't mean a reactionary state." Of course, the reactionary Republican organization will not be happy with our decision. "We can be
equally certain that our return to the Republican party will
bring cheer and encouragement to those Republicans who have
been battling the old guard, as witness the statements of men
like Walter S. Goodland and Sen. Wayne Morse." Besides, the
Republicans are the stronger party in Wisconsin. "My opinion

is that for the present Progressives of Wisconsin can advance their cause most effectively within the Republican party."[50]

After La Follette's speech everything was anticlimactic. Many of the delegates had come with the simple instruction to follow La Follette's lead, whatever that might be. Two hundred and eighty-four voted to join the Republicans. Seventy-seven diehards voted to maintain the Progressive party. Fifty-one voted to take the Progressives into the Democratic ranks. Three preferred the Socialists. Support for the minority positions came from all over the state. Yet, of the fifty-one votes for the Democratic party, twenty-five came from Kenosha, Racine, and Milwaukee, the major areas of labor strength; the Political Action Committee of the C.I.O. had captured these delegations. Of the other twenty-six votes, eighteen came from the sparsely populated counties in the northern half of the state. Of the seventy-seven votes for retaining the Progressive party, twenty-seven came from Milwaukee. The other fifty were scattered throughout the state, often coming from the smaller counties.[51]

"As predicted, it was strictly a case of the convention delegates following Sen. La Follette's lead," a Republican reporter wrote.[52] In many cases this was so. The chairman of the Polk County delegation carried these instructions to Portage: keep the Progressive party alive if at all possible, yet, if it is necessary to join either major party, then join the Democrats, but, above all, follow La Follette's instructions.[53] Polk County's six votes went to the Republican party. Though La Follette had assured the final decision, bitterness and a sense of great disappointment permeated the armory after the vote was taken. Many voted to join the Republicans only at La Follette's insistence, and with a realization of the futility of doing otherwise. With La Follette abandoning his own party, it could only sputter along and die a slower death if others tried to keep it alive. It would be sheer folly for the Progressive party to pit a candidate against Republican La Follette. The convention had not been a happy affair. The delegates were forced to recognize that the party they started with such optimism and enthusiasm twelve years before had now run its course.

Why had the Progressive party run its course? Without

national candidates a state party has never long remained in power. The Progressive party had been unable to extend its influence beyond the borders of Wisconsin. It had been relatively unified by its position on domestic issues, but these issues had been eclipsed by the war. The basic question of foreign policy which the war brought to the surface—what should be America's role in the world?—had split the party. During the war the Progressives could hope only to prevent a further decline in their strength. If the party did this, then, after the war, it could re-establish its position within Wisconsin, and extend its influence beyond the state, establishing itself as a new national party on the chaos and unrest that would follow in the wake of the post-war depression. The election of 1942, and particularly the election of 1944, had shown that the Progressive party had not even been able to hold its own position. And the post-war depression had not come. The Progressive party remained a party of domestic issues in a world which was now more concerned than ever before with international problems. Furthermore, the heavy Democratic vote of 1944 demonstrated that the Wisconsin Democratic party was undercutting much of the Progressive strength, particularly in the industrial areas.

In the years after 1938 the Republican party became easily the dominant party in Wisconsin. Also, after 1938 the Progressive party lacked effective leadership. Robert M. La Follette, Jr., after his 1940 victory, devoted a minimum amount of time to the Progressive party. After 1942 upstate party leaders felt particularly abandoned by him.[54] Orland Loomis had not been able to fill the leadership gap left by the La Follettes. The party was "from its birth . . . a family party—the La Follette party" one Progressive wrote.[55] When the La Follettes left the helm, the party drifted aimlessly. With no effective leadership, and with a war going on, the party organization decayed on the county level; as Senator La Follette pointed out to the Portage Convention, there were party tickets in less than a dozen counties in 1944. When, in preparation for 1946, he was unable to line up suitable candidates, chairman Roberts knew that the party was dead.[56] Enthusiasm for the cause had diminished on the local level, perhaps because the seeds of enthusiasm had not been planted from above. In

April, 1943, Aldric Revell wrote "that the trouble with the party leaders is that they never want to hold a convention where the mass of Progressives could express their opinions."[57] The Progressives had had only three conventions: the convention which founded the party in 1934, the convention which killed the party in 1946, and the convention in Milwaukee in May, 1944. The rank and file of the party workers had lost the fire and the determination and the sense of purpose which had sustained them in the 1930's.

Senator La Follette was well aware of many of these factors which had weakened the Progressive party. But why did he decide to enter the Republican rather than the Democratic party? Certainly some Republican Senators, particularly Wayne Morse, George Aiken, and Robert A. Taft, had privately and publicly urged La Follette to do so. "Speaking only for myself," Senator Morse said the summer before, "I happen to be one Republican who hopes Sen. La Follette will return to the Republican party. . . . I think it will be a great loss to the senate of the United States whenever La Follette leaves that chamber."[58] These men were not alone, for nationally prominent Democrats, Alben W. Barkley and A. S. Mike Monroney, among others, had urged La Follette to run for re-election in their party.[59] Even President Truman reportedly pleaded with La Follette to join the Democrats.[60]

La Follette was, no doubt, flattered by all this attention. Yet the overriding factor in his decision was an appraisal of the political realities as he saw them. Wisconsin had always been a Republican state, and in 1946 the state seemed safely Republican for years to come. Progressive principles were only one side of the coin, La Follette suggested; the other side was to get elected so as to implement those principles. La Follette's own election-winning machine had broken down; the Republican vehicle seemed to be the best means to electoral success. It was fortunate for La Follette that the Democratic party under President Truman seemed to be following a more conservative path, that Truman's programs had met with stiff Congressional resistance, and that Truman had made some major appointments that were anathma to the liberals and progressives when he chose Edwin F. Pauley as Assistant Secretary of the Navy and George Allen to the Reconstruction Finance Corporation. "President Truman is making it more and more difficult for Progressives of the nation to support him with any degree of enthusiasm, not to mention firm and clear conviction," *The Capital Times* said editorially.[61] Progressives of Wisconsin could remember back to the 1930's when they had controlled the state government; at that time the Democrats in the Legislature usually had joined with the Republicans to oppose Progressive measures. This gave La Follette factual material with which to condemn the Democrats and justify his choice of the Republican party. Yet, whatever reasons he advanced to make the Republicans shine more virtuously than the Democrats was probably a rationalization of the course he would have chosen in any case. In March, 1946, it appeared to most observers that La Follette could not be reelected as a Progressive or as a Democrat. Most agreed, however, that he would probably be nominated and re-elected with ease as a Republican.

Most observers agreed that La Follette's only chance for re-election was on the Republican ticket, but there were a few dissenters. Most of the seventy-seven diehards who voted to retain the Progressive party probably believed that La Follette could be re-elected on that ticket. Many of these men had not yet given up on the idea of a national Progressive party. "Everywhere I went," Carey McWilliams wrote in December, 1945, "I found evidence that pointed pretty conclusively to the likelihood of a third-party movement, if not in 1946, then in 1948. With so much 'third-party talk' in the air, the question of what the La Follettes will do in Wisconsin acquires national importance."[62] Thomas L. Stokes, in an article about the Portage Convention, also reported that sentiment in the nation seemed to be growing steadily for a new party.[63] If this indeed were so, many Wisconsin Progressives would want to be in a position to aid and join this movement. They did not want to abandon their own party too soon.

One-half of the votes at Portage for joining the Democratic party came from the industrial areas of Kenosha, Racine, and Milwaukee. The Political Action Committee of the C.I.O. had captured the Progressive delegations in Racine and Kenosha. In Wisconsin in 1946, organized labor wanted to operate within the Democratic party. Their efforts to lure La Follette into the Democratic party proved unavailing. After the Portage Convention these Democrats and labor leaders forgot their words of praise for him and dismissed him as just another Republican. They now turned their efforts to electing their own man, Howard J. McMurray, to the United States Senate. For this reason they hoped to see La Follette defeated in the Republican primary, for they figured that the Republican organization candidate—whoever he might be—would be easier for McMurray to defeat in November. Moreover, Wisconsin Democrats and labor leaders wanted La Follette defeated because he was a Republican, and as a popular Republican his vote-getting power probably would draw in many other Republicans on the Congressional district and County level. For precisely these reasons the national Republican organization was overjoyed at the Portage decision. Senator La Follette would help elect Republicans in Wisconsin who might otherwise face defeat. Liberal Republican Senators Morse and Aiken expressed pleasure to have La Follette in their ranks; so did Senator Bourke Hickenlooper.

Republicans who did not want the Progressives, Democrats who did, and Progressives who did not want to abandon their party—all accused La Follette of political expediency and opportunism or whatever other political sin they could find. "Their shift is not to the Republican party," Thomas E. Coleman said. "It is to the Republican primary. Pure expediency is the motive."[64] A disenchanted Progressive looked at the corpse of his once-beloved party and cried that it was nothing short of murder. "When the verdict is reached," William T. Evjue said, "the *Capital Times* believes that indictments will be returned against Philip F. and Robert M. La Follette, Jr., on the charge that they killed the party by kidnapping it into the realm of opportunism and political expediency. The trouble with the Progressive movement, since the death of the elder La Follette, has been that it was too much La Follette and too little Progressive." Expediency—the desire to re-elect Senator La Follette—had ruled the day. "The great majority of liberals in Wisconsin want Bob La Follette returned to the United States Senate because of the distinguished record he has made there. The *Capital Times* announces now that it will vigorously support Bob La Follette's candidacy for re-election."[65]

With the decision made at Portage, Senator La Follette appeared in a strong position as the lines were drawn for the 1946 campaign. A *New York Times* correspondent pointed out that the Republican organization would do all in its power to defeat La Follette. "The La Follette supporters, and most Wisconsin newsmen, are confident, however, that the Senator will be nominated and re-elected."[66]

A young circuit judge from Shawano added his evaluation to the dissolution of the Progressive party: "The party history of the La Follette brothers (Robert and Phil) is one of successive and successful party destruction. Twelve years ago they temporarily wrecked the Republican party. Then, by playing with the New Dealers in Washington, they wrecked the Democratic party in Wisconsin. They now allow their own child— the Progressive party—to die. And they are about to attempt their fourth wrecking job."

"Personally, as a candidate," Joseph R. McCarthy concluded, "I am glad to see Bob come over and fight in my own back yard. I can assure him that the fight will be very rough, but clean."[67]

Chapter VI

THE DEFEAT OF THE PROGRESSIVES

Joseph Raymond McCarthy was born in Outagamie County, Wisconsin, on November 14, 1908, and there, on a farm, he spent the early years of his life. In August, 1936, McCarthy, then a young lawyer, was elected President of the Young Democratic clubs of Wisconsin's Seventh Congressional district; later that fall he became the Democratic candidate for District Attorney of Shawano County. Nineteen thirty-six was to be the Progressive party's banner year in Wisconsin, and in Shawano County the Progressive candidate defeated McCarthy. Less than three years later McCarthy achieved his first political success when he was elected judge of Wisconsin's Tenth Circuit, comprising Shawano, Outagamie, and Langlade Counties. At thirty he was the youngest judge in the state. In the summer of 1942 Judge McCarthy entered the Marine Corps, and was commissioned as a first lieutenant.

Two years later Senator Alexander Wiley was a candidate for re-election, and McCarthy, now a Marine captain, challenged him in the Republican primary. Armed forced regulations prevented Captain McCarthy from speaking on political issues, so any campaign in his behalf had to be conducted by his friends. In the month before the August primary, McCarthy received a thirty-day leave from the Marines and spent his time in Wisconsin. He insisted that, of course, he was not campaigning, but he did visit and speak to groups of friends throughout the state; such a display of friendship certainly did no harm to the campaign being waged in his behalf. Mc-

Carthy emphasized the fact that he was not campaigning for
the simple reason that he was not allowed to do so. "I wish
I could discuss the importance of oil and the importance of
maintaining a strong army and navy to be used in the event
any international organization breaks down," he told the Milwaukee League of Women Voters, "but I may not do so."[1] Because of the military regulations, and because of the Marine
captain's activity in Wisconsin prior to the primary, Mc-
Carthy's campaign raised several questions of impropriety.
William T. Evjue, as was his custom, commented:

> Perhaps you have been wondering where all the
> money is coming from to finance the expensive cam-
> paign being put on in behalf of the candidacy of Capt.
> Joseph R. McCarthy of the U.S. marines for the Repub-
> lican nomination for United States senator. Military
> regulations prohibit Capt. McCarthy, former circuit
> judge, from participating actively in the campaign,
> but this seems to apply only to making speeches and
> going on the radio. A flood of literature in behalf of
> McCarthy, some of which was prepared at his own
> expense, is being sent out all over the state.[2]

Captain McCarthy did not win the primary—no one really
expected him to win—but he did run a strong race against
Senator Wiley. In a field of four candidates, the Senator won
re-nomination with 153,570 votes, slightly less than half the
Republican total; McCarthy finished second with 79,380 votes.[3]
The fact that he ran so well enhanced his stature for a future
state-wide campaign.

In January, 1945, McCarthy left the Marine Corps and re-
sumed his judicial duties. On December 1, 1945, at a Young
Republican Convention in Milwaukee, Judge McCarthy made
the unsurprising announcement that he would run for the United
States Senate in 1946. In the year before he had traveled
throughout the state and, at the very least, he renewed his
countless friendships. McCarthy knew that he had considerable strength in Wisconsin; now he made it clear that he would
run in the Republican primary with or without the support of
the Republican organization. More than anything else Republican state chairman Thomas E. Coleman wanted to defeat Sen-

ator Robert M. La Follette, Jr., but he did not want to support Judge McCarthy as his candidate against the Senator.[4] At the time of this Young Republican Convention, it was reported that McCarthy met with Coleman in Milwaukee, and Coleman expressed his disinclination to support the young judge in the 1946 campaign. McCarthy replied: "Tom, you're a nice guy and I like you. But I got news for you. When that convention is over next year, Joe McCarthy will be the Republican-endorsed candidate for U.S. Senator."[5]

The Republican Voluntary Committee had been organized by the conservative Republicans in the 1920's when the La Follette Progressives controlled the legal Republican party machinery. The Voluntary Committee was an unofficial, an extra-legal political organization; in contrast was the official, the legally established state central committee. After 1934, when the La Follette Progressives abandoned the Republican party and its official state central committee, the conservatives found that they could still use the Voluntary Committee. First, it enabled them to avoid the limitations which the state corrupt practices act imposed upon campaign expenditures, for these limitations applied only to the official party organization. Second, the Voluntary Committee could support candidates in the primary, while the official state central committee had to remain neutral.

In every election year the Voluntary Committee held a convention, and it was this convention which would endorse candidates that the committee would support in the Republican primary. Yet, the question constantly arose within the Republican party whether it was wise or desirable for the convention to endorse candidates in the first place. In 1942 and 1944 this issue provoked considerable controversy, but both times, the advocates of convention endorsement, under Coleman's leadership, prevailed. In 1946 the issue again arose and produced disharmony within Republican ranks. To Coleman, the necessity for convention endorsement of candidates was clearer than ever before. He had failed in his attempt to have the state Legislature bar Senator La Follette from the Republican primary; now the only way to defeat him, Coleman realized, was for the Republican Voluntary Committee to endorse a candidate and support that one man against La Follette in the primary. It did not matter so much whom the committee endorsed—it could be almost anyone—just so the committee endorsed someone. "The Progressive party leaders do not want us to endorse," Coleman said, "because they want to edge into office under false colors in a primary where several real Republicans would divide their voting strength."[6] In the months before the Republican Convention, Judge McCarthy concentrated his efforts on removing all other serious contenders for the convention endorsement. "Only one man, Circuit Judge Joseph McCarthy of Appleton, is in the field against Bob La Follette," wrote Miles McMillin, a pro-La Follette reporter. "No other serious possibility looms."[7]

The convention of the Republican Voluntary Committee met on May 4th and 5th in Oshkosh. "Sen. La Follette, although he won't be at Oshkosh," Aldric Revell observed, "will be the dominating personality at that convention and he will be the yardstick against which all decisions will be measured."[8] First the convention had to decide whether it would endorse candidates for the primary. Governor Goodland opposed convention endorsement, as he had done in previous years. Coleman again led the fight for endorsement, but uncharacteristically, he spoke to the convention. The following sentence was in the prepared text of his address: "They [the voters] cannot know as we know who might be the men that can best represent our party as candidates and who can best serve as our public officials." Coleman omitted this sentence from the address when he delivered it, but many La Follette supporters used the quotation against Coleman during the campaign to demonstrate his lack of faith in Wisconsin's great institution, the direct primary.[9] One pro-La Follette Republican at the convention has recalled that "there was a definite division among the Conservatives at the Oshkosh convention on the question of welcoming the Progressives back into the Republican party."[10] Part of the opposition to convention endorsement stemmed from a feeling that endorsement would be politically unwise, for Senator La Follette would probably win in the primary anyway; besides, with his vote-getting ability, he would be an asset to Wisconsin Republicans. Furthermore, his experience and connections in Washington were often beneficial to conservative Wisconsin businessmen, and many of them did not want to see him defeated. But when the issue of convention endorsement of candidates came to a vote, Coleman prevailed by a margin of 2,046 to 744 votes. As in 1942 and 1944, the Voluntary Committee would endorse candidates for the primary.

Now, the two most important endorsements facing the convention were for United States Senator and for Governor. In the preceding months Coleman had not become more enthusiastic about Judge McCarthy, but he knew that McCarthy would run with or without the support of the convention. Coleman was disturbed by McCarthy's background as a Democrat, he doubted that McCarthy would be the best vote-getter that the Voluntary Committee could pit against Senator La Follette, and he probably would have preferred to support Walter J. Kohler, Jr., (son of Wisconsin's Governor from 1929 to 1931);[11] yet, under the circumstances, Coleman saw no satisfactory alternative to supporting the young judge. A reluctant Republican convention bestowed its endorsement upon Joseph R. McCarthy. The formal vote was not even close: Perry J. Stearns, an unknown Milwaukee lawyer, was McCarthy's only real opponent, and he received but 298 votes to McCarthy's 2,328; one wayward delegate had the temerity to vote for La Follette. Though a few months before the brash young judge had acted with such impertinence in the presence of the Republican state leader, now this leader's organization was fully committed to the judge's candidacy.

The primary race for Governor would prove to have a decisive effect on the race for Senator. For the convention to endorse Goodland would have been a shrewd political move. It would have put the Republican organization behind an almost certain winner, and it might have effectively undercut a Goodland-La Follette alliance. Yet, Coleman was bitter toward the Governor, and he saw that Goodland's support was tainted because much of it was Progressive; he opposed giving the Governor the convention's blessing. Goodland had many partisans at Oshkosh, and they tried to get the convention to endorse him. The first ballot failed to settle the issue; on the second, the Republicans found a singularly colorless personality, Delbert J. Kenny, and bestowed upon him the convention's endorsement for Governor, a reward for years of loyal party service. This reward seemed ever so nominal, for

virtually all observers gave him no chance for a primary victory.

The Republicans left their Oshkosh Convention in low
spirits. The tide was running strongly Republican throughout
the nation; after 1936 the popular Roosevelt's margins became
increasingly slender and now, in 1946, the unpopular Truman
occupied the White House. The nation was running headlong
to "normalcy" and to Republicanism. Wisconsin Republicans
wanted to hop aboard the national bandwagon, but the organization had given its support to two candidates who seemed
destined to lose to the state's two most popular political personalities—Senator La Follette and Governor Goodland. In
the wake of a La Follette-Goodland triumph, chairman Coleman and his supporters would lose control of the Wisconsin
Republican party. So widespread was the dissatisfaction with
the McCarthy-Kenny slate within the Republican Voluntary
Committee that, in the middle of May, the Republicans held
two secret meetings to consider a new ticket,[12] substituting
Walter J. Kohler, Jr. for McCarthy. Judge McCarthy would
never have withdrawn; Kohler refused to run because, as he
said years later, he did not want to split the Republican party.[13]
These efforts to replace McCarthy, though unsuccessful, indicated the dissatisfaction with the young circuit judge and
the feeling that he simply could not win.

Since 1943, Governor Goodland had done little to dis-
please the Progressives, he had shown no inclination to support McCarthy, and he appeared favorable to Senator La Follette's bid for re-election. The lines were clearly drawn between McCarthy and Kenny on one side and La Follette and
Goodland on the other. Neither Goodland nor La Follette had
yet made any public statements about the candidacy of the
other, but a tacit alliance seemed established; perhaps as
the campaign progressed each would formally endorse the
other. Yet, these clear lines were soon blurred beyond recog-
nition.

Governor Goodland had suggested to General Ralph M.
Immell as early as November, 1945, that Immell run for Governor with Goodland's active support. Between that time and
March 15, 1946, when Goodland unexpectedly announced his
candidacy for re-election, Immell had laid the plans for his

own campaign. Now the Governor asked Immell to be his running-mate for Lieutenant Governor. Immell refused; the notion
of running for Governor, which Goodland had first placed in
his head, now held such an appeal for him that he could not
bear to turn back.[14] A few days after the Republican Convention at Oshkosh, General Immell entered the race for Governor,
but he made no mention of Senator La Follette in his announcement.   He confined himself to state issues, he insisted that
his candidacy was not linked with anyone else's, and he attacked Governor Goodland's administration.   With Immell's
entrance in the campaign many La Follette supporters faced a
dilemma: should they support the General or the Governor?
In his three years as Governor, Goodland had endeared himself to the Progressives, and he seemed to merit their support.
Immell, however, was a long-time La Follette friend and a
loyal Progressive of many years standing.   Some La Follette
supporters favored Goodland, others favored Immell.   Senator
La Follette would draw support from both camps;   his best
course lay in neutrality.

       The Republican Convention did not signal the beginning
of Judge McCarthy's campaign—it had been going on for several months—but it did bring to the surface an issue which
had been raised against him.   Article VII, Section 10 of the
Wisconsin Constitution prohibits state circuit and supreme
court judges from running for any other office in the following words:

>   They shall hold no office of public trust, except
> a judicial office, during the term for which they are
> respectively elected, and all votes for either of them
> for any office, except a judicial office, given by the
> legislature or the people, shall be void.

McCarthy's supporters claimed that the state constitution
could not establish the qualifications for any national office,
like United States Senator.   In a letter to state Republican
leaders, chairman Coleman defended McCarthy against these
charges: "Consider the attempt of La Follette supporters to
make an issue by demanding the resignation of a circuit judge,
who entered the marines as a private, gave up his judicial income for that period, was honorably discharged as a captain,

and has no lush outside income to match that of the senator [through his interest in radio station WEMP]. . . . no clause in any state constitution applies to a candidate for the United States senate."[15]   After announcing his candidacy, McCarthy said that "the constitution of the United States, not the constitution of Wisconsin, establishes the qualifications of members of the U.S. senate."[16]   The judge-in-politics issue provided handy ammunition to those who would oppose McCarthy in any case; *The Capital Times* constantly charged that McCarthy's candidacy was both unethical and illegal.   "Judge McCarthy is flouting a well established principle of political ethics if he continues to campaign without resigning his present judgeship,"[17] the *Times* said. *The Milwaukee Journal* also questioned McCarthy's candidacy on these grounds. "The McCarthy candidacy," the *Journal* stated, "is in violation of at least the spirit of provisions in both the Wisconsin constitution and the Wisconsin statutes—provisions intended to keep the judiciary out of partisan politics."[18]   The La Follette supporters did not take any legal action against McCarthy before the primary, perhaps because, as one of them later suggested, they did not take McCarthy's campaign as a serious threat to the Senator.[19]

Judge McCarthy's campaign consisted of three major elements: first, his military record;   second, an attack upon the New Deal; and third, an attack upon Senator La Follette. McCarthy's greatest asset was the simple fact that he was a war veteran.   He campaigned as a humble war hero, a "tail-gunner" who was seriously wounded in the service of his country. In 1946 any young veteran was a national hero and a potentially popular candidate for political office.   The political value of a military record had long been apparent. In the years after the Civil War, a combat record became an unquestioned political asset.   The Spanish American War gave us a future President.   Twenty years later Franklin D. Roosevelt realized that an active military role would give a boost to his own political career; perhaps somewhere in France he would find his own San Juan Hill. After the Second World War the value of a military record for a political candidate was at its premium; never before had a military conflict so unified the nation and been so dramatic and so immediately important to the American people. Nineteen forty-six was the year of the veteran in politics, and McCarthy climbed aboard the bandwagon. In actual fact, he had not served in combat, let alone as a tail-gunner, but in 1946, this was not widely known; furthermore, it was sacrilege to challenge a veteran's veracity. Joe McCarthy pointed out that it was the Joe McCarthys who had won the war for America. "JOE McCARTHY was a TAIL GUNNER in World War II," a newspaper ad said. "TODAY JOE McCARTHY IS HOME. He wants to SERVE America in the SENATE. Yes, folks, CONGRESS NEEDS A TAIL GUNNER."[20]

Republicans in Wisconsin sensed a rising anti-New Deal trend. In 1944, for the first time, Roosevelt had failed to carry Wisconsin, and, since Truman became President, the standing of the New Deal had fallen still further. Judge McCarthy looked upon the Democratic administration with the horror to be expected from Republicans, and he repeatedly labeled La Follette a "New Deal Senator" in words such as these:

> Mr. La Follette, the gentleman from Virginia, and his group are staking their political futures on the hope that all of the honest labor vote, all of the honest labor leaders, can be wrapped up and delivered to them by the few selfish, self-proclaimed, misnamed labor leaders from whom the New Dealers and La Follette have been taking orders. . . .
>
> If, however, the gentlemen from Virginia is right, if the great masses of votes can be packaged and delivered, then the group that is now in power shall finish the job which they have begun. They shall do what no enemy from without has ever been able to do with this country. They shall destroy this nation from within.[21]

Later in the campaign McCarthy said, in a series of charges against the Senator, "that by your failure to do anything to promote industrial peace you are playing into the hands of the communists."[22] McCarthy also assailed "Sen. La Follette's anti-farm record."[23] He condemned Senator La Follette for failing "to do a single thing to prepare us for World War II, with failing to take part in intelligent post-war planning and with failing to seek legislation aimed at providing war veterans with homes. . . . What Sen. La Follette and other New Dealers have done to the country has become so obvious since the war ended that we need not discuss that."[24]

During his career in the Senate, and especially during the war, Young Bob La Follette had seldom returned to Wisconsin. This helped to create the impression that the Senator was aloof from the people of Wisconsin and their problems, that he was a Washington Senator rather than a Wisconsin Senator. One reporter said that Senator La Follette, "over a period of years in Washington, seemed to grow aloof from the people down in the local precincts of the state he represented."[25] Judge McCarthy, in obvious contrast, conducted a highly personal campaign, traveling throughout the state, everywhere shaking hands and making speeches. In addition, McCarthy conducted an extensive campaign through the mail, sending out reams of literature showing him in his marine uniform. In the last days of the campaign hundreds of thousands of post-cards, handwritten by a staff of women, flooded the state. Judge McCarthy constantly referred to La Follette as "the Gentleman from Virginia," the country squire in the East who no longer cared for Wisconsin. Senator La Follette had once owned a small and run-down house in Virginia, a house in which he never lived and which he had sold years before 1946; he owned and lived in a modest house in the District of Columbia.

The Republican Voluntary Committee vigorously supported Judge McCarthy's campaign. In contrast to the relatively unorganized campaign for Senator La Follette, the Republican organization operated smoothly. The Committee to Elect Joseph R. McCarthy and the Voluntary Committee spent approximately $50,000 on the campaign; La Follette reported expenditures of only $3,728.[26] In late 1945 state chairman Coleman had made frequent attacks on Senator La Follette's interest in Milwaukee radio station WEMP. This campaign continued; in the summer a half-page ad appeared in Wisconsin's major newspapers asking "How Did La Follettes Get That Money?"[27] McCarthy himself often raised this question. The issue greatly annoyed La Follette, though he did not discuss it publicly. La Follette believed that there was no conflict of interest in his holdings in WEMP and his senatorial duties, and he resented the implication that there was. Coleman had shrewdly raised the issue of special privilege against the name long associated with the fight against special privilege. The organization's attacks on the Senator did not stop with station WEMP. In a letter to the party faithful, Coleman said that Senator La Follette is the man

> who is more responsible for the confusion in this nation today than any other single person in the senate.
>
> Go back to the days of La Follette's Civil Liberties committee and you will find all the evidence that you need to prove that he is the man who promoted the class hatred that the New Deal has nurtured for 14 years.
>
> Go back through the New Deal administration of government and you will find La Follette trotting along with it on practically every evil that it promoted.
>
> Examine his record and you will find no evidence that he realizes that farmers are the great bulwark of Wisconsin's citizens. He has ignored them until election time in the same manner that he has always forgotten Wisconsin between campaigns.[28]

A few weeks after the Republican Convention, the Voluntary Committee distributed five major pieces of literature, three of them on McCarthy's candidacy. One of these pamphlets pointed with great pride to McCarthy's sacrifices during World War II in waiving his judicial salary, and asked: "Did the Progressive senator who returns to the state only intermittently from his estate in Virginia, chiefly for campaign purposes, make any sacrifice at all?"[29] So badly did Thomas E. Coleman and the Voluntary Committee want to defeat La Follette that on this contest hinged the control of the Wisconsin Republicans; McCarthy's victory could, for several years at least, keep the La Follette Progressives from posing as a serious threat to conservative control of the party.

Before the Portage Convention the state Democrats attempted to draw Senator La Follette into their party, but it was fairly obvious that they would not succeed. One month before that convention, Aldric Revell wrote that "Democrats, as soon after Mar. 17 as feasible, will begin trotting out their

candidates and it will be interesting to note that the same
Democratic politicians, now beseiging Sen. La Follette to come
into their party, will be lambasting him for imaginary short-
comings when he decides to keep out of the Democratic ranks."[30]
After that convention, the Democrats did indeed discover that
there were many things wrong with La Follette, many reasons
why he should be replaced in the Senate by a true Democrat.
On domestic issues, the Democrats charged, La Follette's old
liberal fire had disappeared. It is true that in the 1930's he
had sponsored unemployment relief, public works beyond Harry
Hopkins' wildest dreams, and his committee on civil liberties
had done a great service to organized labor, but these crusading fires of old were now burned out, for in recent years
Senator La Follette had not initiated any significant liberal
legislation. Yet, their heaviest blows hammered at his record
on foreign policy. By his actions before Pearl Harbor, by his
political speech of May, 1944, and his Senate speech of May,
1945, Senator La Follette had demonstrated that he was an
isolationist, a dirty word to Wisconsin Democrats. To add
further substance to their charge, in the spring of 1946 Senator La Follette had come out against the four billion dollar
loan to Great Britain.

Yet, despite their criticisms of La Follette's record on
domestic and foreign affairs, the Democrats' major objection
to the Senator was not based on substantive issues. The
Democrats opposed La Follette because he was now a Republican. His popularity would pull other Republicans to victory who otherwise would be defeated. "If Bob La Follette
should be nominated on the Republican ticket," Thomas R. Amlie told the University of Wisconsin Young Democrats, "this
fact will help elect all the reactionaries who are sure to be
nominated on the Republican ticket."[31] Because of his popularity, and because of his record on domestic issues, the
Democrats had wanted La Follette to join their ranks; now that
he placed his popular name on the Republican ticket, they opposed him. Their strong showing in 1944 had convinced the
Democrats that they could be a major political force within
Wisconsin, even to the extent of winning occasional elections. With organized labor supporting them, and with liberal
candidates such as Hoan and McMurray, they believed they

could inherit much of the Progressive following.   In their attempt to become the instrument of liberal action in Wisconsin, the Democrats saw that Progressive Republican La Follette was a major threat.   They hoped for his defeat in the
Republican primary, for they could more easily defeat a conservative Republican, like McCarthy, in the general election.
In a contest between Democrat Howard J. McMurray and Republican McCarthy, the Democrats hoped that the La Follette
Progressives would support McMurray and the entire Democratic ticket.   This was a forlorn hope; in the primary campaign, Democratic attacks upon La Follette were so intense
and so bitter that they alienated a large amount of possible
Progressive support.   "One group a few months ago was lav-
ishly praising my record and inviting me to join forces with
them," La Follette said towards the end of the primary campaign.   "Now they are trying hard to place their mental processes in reverse and find something to attack in my record."[32]

In recalling his attempt to persuade La Follette to run for
re-election as a Democrat, McMurray added: "I also told the
Senator that if he ran as a Republican, I would file as a Democratic candidate and remove him from the United States Senate.   He shrugged his shoulders and said 'Do you think you
can do that?' I answered 'Certainly.'"[33] If McMurray's rec-
ollection of this meeting is correct, then he must be reckoned
a man of his word.   In early May he announced his candidacy
for the Senate, and ran unopposed for the Democratic nomination.   He received strong labor support, and *The Wisconsin
CIO News* gave extensive coverage to his campaign.   From
that time on McMurray waged a pre-primary campaign as vigorous and as an extensive as McCarthy's, and, like McCarthy,
he directed his attack against Senator La Follette.   He tried
to identify La Follette with reactionary Republicans, and to
make him responsible for his brothers in political arms.   In
one radio speech McMurray spent a great amount of time de-
nouncing Senator Robert A. Taft, and he read a letter in which
Taft endorsed La Follette for re-election.   He spent so much
time on the Ohio Senator, McMurray explained, because "Senator Taft is supporting Senator Robert M. La Follette, Jr. in
his campaign for re-nomination on the Republican ticket in
Wisconsin."[34] As primary day approached and his attacks on

La Follette became sharper and broader in scope, McMurray said: "The record will show that Bob has voted for labor's interest about half of the time, but investigation brings out the all important fact that he has quit fighting for liberal causes."[35]

Judge McCarthy occasionally touched on foreign affairs. "Senator La Follette is playing into the hands of the Communists by opposing world co-operation," he said at one point,[36] yet this was a minor part of his anti-New Deal campaign. In contrast, McMurray's attacks on La Follette's domestic record were secondary to his criticisms of the Senator's position on foreign affairs. He constantly recalled La Follette's opposition to the Roosevelt policies before Pearl Harbor; he could not see "how any of the young men who have returned from fighting this war can consistently support a man who did everything in his power before Pearl Harbor to prevent us from winning that war—nor can the parents of those who fought and died ever forgive that lack of statesmanship of Bob La Follette."[37] McMurray drew attention to La Follette's post-war statements, which seemed to give less support to international co-operation and the United Nations than McMurray favored, and he tried to make the label "isolationist" stick.

Isolationists had a rough time of it in 1946. Senators Henrik Shipstead of Minnesota and Burton K. Wheeler of Montana were defeated in their quest for re-nomination; both had served in the Senate since the early twenties. Former Senator Gerald Nye of North Dakota, who had been defeated in 1944, tried for a political comeback, but he, too, was defeated. On the Sunday before the primary, August 11, the Democrats sponsored a full page ad in Wisconsin's major newspapers. "Good-bye, Isolationists!" ran the headline. The names of Shipstead, Wheeler, Nye, and former Representative Hamilton Fish, Jr. were summarily crossed out. Then followed the proclamation, "Good-bye, La Follette!" The sweeping attack on the Senator touched on his position on price controls and Taft's endorsement, it noted that he had betrayed the Progressives, that he had betrayed President Roosevelt, and that he was sure to betray the Republicans, but the heaviest cannonading was directed to La Follette's isolationism. The concluding item in the advertisement extolled the abundant virtues of Howard J. McMurray.[38]

McMurray contended that President Roosevelt had told him in the spring of 1944 that he wanted to "correct . . . one of my worst mistakes," which was his support in Wisconsin for the Progressives, and defeat Senator La Follette in 1946. "The President was angry because the La Follette brothers were determined to run a Progressive Candidate against me in 1944."[39] "I hope," McMurray said in the closing days of the primary campaign, "the people of Wisconsin will do what the president told me he wanted done."[40] In the same speech, McMurray added that "Nazi and Fascist newspapers" approved of many of La Follette's ideas. "He promoted ideas all the Fascists like, just as they liked the ideas of Burton K. Wheeler."[41] The vigor and bitterness of McMurray's attacks became personal as the campaign drew to a close. "Bob La Follette can skip nimbly from party to party whenever he feels the ground slipping beneath him," McMurray said four days before the primary, "but in one respect he never shifts. He never changes his lifelong slogan, 'I am for me.'"[42]

In the years after 1950 Joseph R. McCarthy became a national personality in his own right, and anti-McCarthyites looked with dismay upon the 1946 campaign which hoisted this young judge to the Senate over the venerated Robert M. La Follette, Jr. In hunting for a scapegoat for the crime of '46, many of them pointed an accusing finger at none other than the Communists, and, with supreme confidence, proclaimed, "The Communists—they did it! They were out to get La Follette, and they got him good! They defeated him by supporting McCarthy." *The Progressive*, the direct heir of the La Follette's family magazine, put this case very well: "The Communists, furious at La Follette because he was even than warning his countrymen of the expansionist ambitions of Soviet imperialism, threw their support to McCarthy."[43] Jack Anderson and Ronald May, who wrote a book on McCarthy in 1952, took the same position and concluded: "So they [the Communist leaders of the state C.I.O.] cranked out reams of hate-La Follette literature and rallied the workers behind McCarthy. When Joe was asked by reporters about this, he said: 'Communists have the same right to vote as anyone else, don't they?'"[44] Such a charge, if true, had an understandable appeal to McCarthy's opponents. It did contain just enough truth to seem completely substantial to those who wanted to believe it.

The specific charge was that the Communists controlled the Wisconsin C.I.O., that the state C.I.O. betrayed La Follette, labor's loyal friend, and stabbed him in the back in 1946 because, after June 22, 1941, he had opposed aid to Russia, and because, in 1944 and 1945, he had said a number of nasty things about the Soviet Union. The Communists and fellow-travelers were knocked out of power at a state C.I.O. convention in December, 1946. The new state C.I.O. President, Herman Steffes, said years later: "The Communists definitely were responsible for the election of McCarthy. We did all we could to offset Communists in the state and Milwaukee councils but were outnumbered." Aware that Senator McCarthy faced re-election in 1952, Steffes added: "We have to redeem ourselves now."[45] Three principal leaders have been pointed to as the leading Communists in the state C.I.O.: Melvin Heinritz, state secretary-treasurer, "whom the Milwaukee *Journal* identified as a Communist," Harold Christoffel, "outstanding Wisconsin Communist" of Local 248 of the United Auto Workers at the Allis Chalmers plant near Milwaukee,[46] and Meyer Adleman, a member of the state C.I.O. executive board. These leaders dominated the state C.I.O. and its 75,000 members.

Senator La Follette had delivered a speech at the Progressive party convention in Milwaukee in May, 1944, a speech widely recognized as isolationist. One year later, on the floor of the Senate, La Follette delivered one of the most important speeches of his career. In this three-hour discourse on foreign policy, he expressed doubts that the United Nations would be or could be effective in solving post-war problems. "I feel a deepening apprehension that the purpose, program, and possibilities of the [San Francisco] Conference have been oversold to the American people, and doubtless to other peoples of the world," Senator La Follette said. "It has become virtually impossible to criticize the activities of at least one of our allies—Soviet Russia—however constructively, without bringing down about one's head a storm of smearing vilification and misrepresentation by a tightly organized minority in the United States." Russia's "present demands and her methods seem more in accord with the old imperialistic purposes and methods of the czarist regime than with those of the early days of her revolution. . . . Russia's policies in Europe have constituted a direct violation of the pledges of the Atlantic Charter, to which she subscribed." The most important case of this is Poland, but it is also true in the case of Rumania, Bulgaria, Hungary and Austria; Russia obviously has violated the recent Yalta agreement. "This agreement has been consistently flouted by the Soviet Union, which has proceeded unilaterally, and without in any way consulting her two partners, namely the United States and Great Britain, to set up in country after country governments which are made in Moscow, and do not fulfill any of the basic requirements agreed to at Yalta. . . . the fundamental fact is always the same— Russia ignores her solemn commitments made at Yalta to a program of joint responsibility and cooperation in establishing temporary regimes for the liberated lands of Europe." Russia's recent actions also grossly violate "the democratic principles which can alone provide a political climate for enduring peace." Senator La Follette pointed out that he was not condemning just the Soviet Union, that he was just as unhappy with British rule over India, Burma, and Malta as with Russian domination of Eastern Europe. Yet, he directed the brunt of his attack against the Soviet Union. "I believe that from the beginning our conduct has been too much predicated on the theory that it was essential to get Russia into this organization, and that the concessions which have been made at the conferences, and especially at Yalta—so far as we know them—were a mistake."[47]

Senator La Follette's speeches on foreign policy in May, 1944, and May, 1945, provoked an intensive attack by the state C.I.O. *The Wisconsin CIO News* pursued a strongly internationalist line, lauding our great Soviet ally and expressing gratification at the co-operation between Great Britain, the United States, and the Soviet Union. After Senator La Follette's Milwaukee speech of May, 1944, the C.I.O. said:

> Under the leadership of defeatist, America First forces, headed by Bob La Follette, Jr., [the Progressive] convention adopted a foreign policy resolution that will tickle the heart of every defeatist in this

land. In his address, La Follette sniped at the leadership of President Roosevelt and did his best to undermine faith in the world agreements made at Teheran
and Moscow.[48]

Aldric Revell, a Progressive reporter, and also President of the
Dane County Industrial Union Council (C.I.O.), wrote to Philip
La Follette late in 1944 that "Labor, instigated by the Communist controlled CIO in Wisconsin, is sour on Bob, not because
of his record, but because of his so-called isolationism."[49]
After La Follette's more important speech of May 31, 1945, the
state C.I.O. unleashed a barrage of criticism against the Senator. The banner headline on the next issue of *The Wisconsin
CIO News* proclaimed: "Blast La Follette Plea for 'Tolerance'
Toward Nazi Germany, Fascist Leaders." In the article state
secretary-treasurer Mel Heinritz deplored La Follette's "denunciation of our great Soviet ally," and continued:

> Senator La Follette is serving notice that he is
> going to spearhead the fight against a World Security
> Organization and blast the people's hopes for peace
> and security.
> Moreover, he fights the only basis upon which the
> World Security Organization can be successful and
> that is in the unity of the Big three. . . .
> Although he inveighs against British imperialism,
> he says no word against the present trend in our for-
> eign policy of cooperating with British imperialism
> against the democratic movements in Europe and
> against the Soviet Union.[50]

In subsequent issues in the summer of 1945, *The Wisconsin
CIO News* took notice that several local C.I.O. unions within
the state had sent letters of protest to Senator La Follette.
One article, which quoted two such letters, ended on the hope-
ful note that peace would be won. "No demagogues are going
to stand in the way. Not even a Senator Bob La Follette."[51]
Another article headlined: "Ask La Follette Deny Links with
Pro-Fascist, Gerald Smith Groups," and ended on the note that
"such groups . . . will have nothing but praise for the 3-hour
Senate speech of Senator Bob La Follette. They could not have

expressed their sentiments any better. In fact, not as well."[52]
One C.I.O. writer viewed with dismay the fact that La Follette
"actually charges that the Soviets are trying to force their
system upon other countries."[53] The campaign which the state
C.I.O. waged against Senator La Follette because of his position on foreign policy was very intensive and very substantial.
La Follette implied in his Senate speech that he would be the
brunt of such a barrage of criticism. He became self-righteous
about these attacks, and felt simply that the labor leaders
were wrong.[54]

The state C.I.O. leaders, however, were not the only ones
to howl in protest to La Follette's Senate speech. *The Wisconsin State Journal*, never recently noted for left-wing ten-
dencies, charged that La Follette had made clear his return to
isolationism, and that his speech was a "sneering, vicious
treatment of the people beside whom this nation has fought
for the chance to make a place for the will to peace possible."[55] His speech was purely political, delivered with 1946
fully in mind. *The Milwaukee Journal* entitled its lead editorial "La Follette Is Destructive." If the Senator's "purpose
is to sabotage the work being done at San Francisco and en-
throne the isolationism" of the post World War I period, "he
could hardly have done better" than his recent Senate speech,
most of which was "devoted to blasting at the nations with
which we must work if there is to be any international collab-
oration against war."[56] In May, 1945, the emphasis in American foreign policy was towards more reliance on the San Francisco Conference and a greater attempt to co-operate with the
Soviet Union than La Follette believed desirable. At that time
the war with Japan was far from over, and the assistance of
the Soviet Union seemed necessary to bring the war in the Far
East to a speedy conclusion. The state C.I.O. was not alone
in its denunciation of the Senator's foreign policy speech; because significant non-Communists questioned the wisdom of
what La Follette said, the C.I.O. charges do not appear especially sinister.

In the months after Senator La Follette's foreign policy
speech of May, 1945, the state C.I.O. attacked him on foreign
policy alone. Then, in the months prior to the Portage Convention, they did not mention him. They were aware that many

labor leaders and Democratic politicians were trying to persuade La Follette to join their party; perhaps they were waiting
to see which way he jumped, preparing to support him for re-
election if he ran as a Democrat. In any case, after the Portage Convention, when La Follette officially cast his lot with
the Republicans, the C.I.O. broadened its attack to include the
Senator's domestic record. In early April the C.I.O. in Milwaukee issued a statement saying that "any claim that La Follette can make to liberal support is now blasted." The statement distorted his record; it implied that La Follette favored
lowering the minimum wage in the bill before Congress from
sixty-five cents per hour to sixty cents, and that La Follette
voted for the farm parity amendment, which would "guarantee"
parity prices to farmers, but which labor opposed because of
its effect on consumer prices for food.[57] Both of these C.I.O.
charges were untrue. A leading A.F.L. paper in Wisconsin
came to La Follette's defense on this question, and added that
"La Follette has been long on the side of the laboring man
during his 20 years in the U.S. Senate."[58] Even the national
C.I.O. entered the fracas; Nathan Cowan, national C.I.O. legislative representative, defended the Senator against the false
charges, and wrote to La Follette: "Please rest assured that
the CIO is highly appreciative of your votes in behalf of recent legislation favored by this organization."[59] As a result
of this episode, Aldric Revell said: "The Communists, who
dominate the Milwaukee county and state CIO executive committees, have launched the expected smear campaign to 'sabotage' U.S. Sen. Robert M. La Follette."[60] A month before the
primary, *The Wisconsin CIO News* carried an editorial entitled "How About it, Bob?" The editorial quoted part of a
letter La Follette had sent to residents of Wisconsin on the
question of price controls. "The Senator, it is clear from the
above [letter], is lukewarm about an OPA with teeth in it which
is the only kind the people want. Further, he falls hook, line
and sinker for the NAM line that the OPA has stifled production." In addition to these sins, La Follette has failed to repudiate Taft's endorsement. "It gives one to think—with
primary day less than a month away."[61]

"I think the workers will vote solidly for Bob," Joseph
Padway, general counsel of the A.F.L., said. "Some, it is true,

differed with him on his war record, but La Follette has had a 20-year record of pro-labor activity and that's what will count at the showdown."[62] The enthusiasm he expressed for La Follette did not extend throughout the state A.F.L.   The United Labor Committee, composed of A.F.L. and C.I.O. unions and railroad brotherhoods, did not aid La Follette. There was "deep seated resentment" because the Senator had failed to consult with them before the Portage Convention as to what political course he should follow.[63]   Peter Schoeman, President of the Milwaukee Building and Construction Trades council, and a leading spokesman for the A.F.L. in Wisconsin, said, "I do not believe that labor should endorse anyone in a Wisconsin primary. . . . Since Wisconsin laws require that one voter can cast his primary election ballot in only one party, an endorsement of Bob La Follette at this time is an endorsement of the entire Republican ticket."[64]   Schoeman's view reflected the attitude of most of the Wisconsin A.F.L. which, though not opposing La Follette, did not lift a finger in his behalf during the primary.

During the 1930's, organized labor's political activity in Wisconsin was drawn in two directions; on the state level labor supported the Progressives but, on the national level, labor supported President Roosevelt and the Democrats. Gradually, the force tending to the Democratic party became stronger and withdrew labor support from the Progressives.   In May, 1942, Orland Loomis wrote to Bob La Follette that "Bill Rubin [a Wisconsin Democrat] and others have spent a lot of time with labor leaders convincing them that the progressives have washed out and that their only hope is with the democratic ticket."[65] During the war, and with the obvious demise of the Progressive party, labor allied itself with the Democrats in Wisconsin. "Since the conflict between Roosevelt and the La Follettes on foreign policy," Aldric Revell wrote in June, 1944, "labor has switched to the Democratic party."[66]   In 1944, labor's commitment to the party of Roosevelt was complete. Organized labor's attack against La Follette paralleled the Democratic campaign by concentrating on substantive issues, domestic and foreign, and, like the Democrats, their major objection to La Follette was altogether different; they opposed him because he was a Republican. As a popular candidate he was likely to contribute to the victory of undesirable and obviously anti-labor Republicans in races for Congressional and state legislative seats. Labor had chosen to operate within the Democratic party, and Howard J. McMurray was a perfect candidate for them.

"The statement of principles of the state Democratic Party," *The Wisconsin CIO News* said, "adopted in convention last weekend, is, in general, based on policies consistent with the aims of the CIO-PAC, both within the state and nationally."[67] The C.I.O. made its greatest efforts in Milwaukee's Fourth Congressional District where it supported Edmund Bobrowicz, a young veteran and a C.I.O. member, against the incumbent Congressman, Democrat Thad Wasliewski. The C.I.O.'s enthusiasm for Bobrowicz was undisguised and unbounded, and its campaign for him was extremely vigorous.[68] Two weeks before the primary, the Milwaukee County C.I.O. endorsed candidates in the primary races for the state Senate and Assembly and Bobrowicz for Congress. All of the candidates endorsed were Democrats, with but two exceptions, and these two Republicans endorsed were C.I.O. members; in both districts where Republican candidates were endorsed, Democratic candidates also were endorsed.[69] Howard J. McMurray has attested to the Democratic-labor alliance by acknowledging that he organized his anti-La Follette campaign in conjunction with labor officials in Kenosha, Racine, and Milwaukee.[70] The Socialist party of Wisconsin explained well why liberal Democrats, labor leaders, and Socialists felt it would be unwise to enter the Republican primary and support Senator La Follette in his campaign against Judge McCarthy:

> A grave blow will be dealt all forward looking legislation if labor and co-operators rush into the Republican primaries to support one or two favorite candidates. If forward looking voters go into the Republican primary to vote for one person, they will necessarily put into office a hundred reactionaries for the single candidate.[71]

In January, 1946, Senator La Follette said that he was "worried" that labor would not follow the Progressives into the Republican party.[72] Organized labor, by supporting Democratic candidates in the primary, drew into the Democratic primary voters who probably would have voted for La Follette if they had entered the Republican primary. It is important to recall that in Wisconsin a person can vote in the primary of only one party, but at every primary election he is perfectly free to choose what party that will be. By urging its partisans to vote in the Democratic primary, therefore, labor directly hurt Senator La Follette. For La Follette, the defection of labor was a serious blow. Labor support had made victory impressive in 1934; in 1940 it alone had made victory possible. For victory in 1946 strong labor support would be essential.

Labor in Wisconsin regarded Senator La Follette's candidacy either with silence (A.F.L.) or with open hostility (C.I.O.). The national C.I.O. was less hostile than the state organization; nevertheless, the Political Action Committee of the C.I.O., in releasing a partial list of the incumbent Senators it supported, and a list of those it opposed for re-election, made no mention of Senator La Follette on either list.[73] Immediately after the primary, Jack Kroll, the new director of the Political Action Committee, said that the committee "took no part" in the La Follette campaign. In view of Senator La Follette's friendship for labor, Kroll was asked, was it not fair to assume that labor would have supported him? "I don't think your assumption is well founded," Kroll replied.[74]

The American Federation of Labor, in marked contrast, warmly supported Senator La Follette. "I heartily endorse the candidacy of Sen. La Follette for nomination and re-election to the United States senate," President William Green wrote to a Wisconsin labor official. "I respectfully urge labor and all the friends of labor in the state of Wisconsin to rally to his support and re-elect him to the U.S. senate by an overwhelming majority."[75] Five railroad brotherhoods joined in his support: "We sincerely endorse the candidacy of Sen. La Follette and respectfully urge every worker in the state to rally to his support for nomination and re-election to the U.S. senate."[76] They devoted an entire four-page issue of their publication *Labor* to the Senator, which they called the "Special La Follette Edition."[77] Tens of thousands of this issue blanketed the state before the primary. National labor leaders responded quite differently from state labor leaders to Senator

La Follette's quest for the Republican Senatorial nomination, for their view, their interests, and their perspective all were different. The national labor leaders were many times quite unaware of the particular, and often peculiar, political circumstances in the various states. For Wisconsin labor leaders, the fact that Senator La Follette ran as a Republican was largely responsible for producing their opposition to him; for national labor leaders it was far less significant than the fact that La Follette was a friend of labor in the United States Senate.

Senator La Follette wanted the whole-hearted support of labor, but he did not get it. He was wary of support from conservative and strongly nationalistic groups, but this support he got. Former Representative Hamilton Fish, in November, 1945, expressed great confidence in the Republican party's flexibility, a party "big enough in its principles to take in all Progressives on a platform mutually agreeable. . . . Sen. La Follette has been a consistent American and no supporter of Communism."[78] At the Republican state convention in May, Lester Bradshaw produced a letter from Senator Robert A. Taft of Ohio, which said in part:

> I hope La Follette is successful. I get on with him very well and would have no difficulty in agreeing with him on social welfare measures. In the long run he will be closer to me than he will be to Morse. Furthermore, Tom Coleman appears to be tied up with Stassen. I don't think La Follette will ever get in that campaign, because he disapproves so strongly of Stassen's foreign policies.[79]

Walter B. Chilsen, editor of *The Merrill Daily Herald*, announced that he would support Senator La Follette, a good American who places the interests of the United States above the interests of other countries.[80]

La Follette was not very concerned about this conservative and nationalistic support if it did not go too far, but eventually it did. In July, the epitome of intolerant nationalism, Gerald L. K. Smith, endorsed the Senator for re-election. "We cannot forget," Smith said, "that the entire La Follette family has always put America first, regardless of any differences of opinion some of our people may have had concerning other matters." Within hours after Smith endorsed him, La Follette replied sharply: "I want to make it as emphatically clear as I can that I absolutely, and without reservation of any kind whatsoever, repudiate the support of Gerald L. K. Smith and any others who preach a gospel of hate and intolerance."[81] However much Senator La Follette may have disliked Smith's support, his position on foreign policy and his strong attacks on the Soviet Union doubtless encouraged it.

This conservative and strongly nationalistic support became a handicap in his campaign for re-election. La Follette's immediate repudiation of Smith's endorsement was a wise political move, but he viewed Taft's support in a much different light. Despite their differences, La Follette and Taft had become close personal friends, and they had great respect for each other. La Follette did not want to offend a friend by repudiating his support. Furthermore, he may have believed that the Taft endorsement would be a political asset. One Republican favorable to La Follette in 1946 has recalled that:

> some of the La Follette people thought it [the Taft endorsement] might bring the voluntary committee group to their senses sufficiently to make them steer away from endorsing anyone and that it might even convince them that it would be a good thing to have people like Senator La Follette in the Republican party. As I now recall, no one on La Follette's side at that time felt the labor people would be stupid enough to condemn a long time supporter of labor, such as Senator La Follette merely because Senator Taft chose to endorse him.[82]

The Taft letter did not bring the Voluntary Committee to its senses, but in the industrial areas it proved to be an albatross around La Follette's neck. The state C.I.O. exploited this issue to the hilt, making La Follette fully responsible for everything that Taft did and stood for. *The Wisconsin CIO News* reprinted an article from the June issue of *The International Teamster*, because the article "raises questions about Senator La Follette which are certainly in the minds of many CIO members in our state." The Teamster article said: "To find Taft supporting La Follette, to the extent of interceding in the convention of another state, is a startling and disturbing incident."[83]   The Democrats also made an issue of Taft's endorsement.   Andrew Biemiller, a former Progressive and, in 1946, the Democratic Congressman from Milwaukee's Fifth District, told the Democratic state convention that "There is a strong rumor in Washington which more than meets the eye in view of the Taft-La Follette endorsement. The deal is that Taft is to support Bob for the senate in 1946 and Bob will support Taft for President in 1948."[84]   Towards the end of the campaign the La Follette camp probably realized that Taft's endorsement was a liability in the industrial and labor areas. An advertisement in *The Milwaukee Journal* nine days before the primary was headlined, like most La Follette ads, "A Senator to Be Proud of!" and it included endorsements from many Senators; noticeably absent were the words of support from Robert A. Taft.[85]

There was no unusual national interest—or lack of interest—in the Wisconsin primary. Because Senator Robert M. La Follette, Jr. had been on the national scene for more than two decades, it was natural that many public figures who knew him in Washington would express the hope that he would be re-elected.   "I think it would be a great loss to Wisconsin, the country, the senate, and the Republican party," Senator Wayne Morse said, "if he should not be returned to continue his great service."[86]   Senator George Aiken voiced similar sentiments, and said that the Progressives' return to the Republican party "is the most encouraging thing that has happened to the Republican party in 12 years."[87] Miles McMillin reported that the famous Taft letter to Lester Bradshaw endorsing La Follette squared with "reports" that the Republican national organization was trying to call Coleman off in his uncompromising opposition to La Follette.[88]   National politicians, like national labor leaders, were many times quite unaware of the particular, and often peculiar, political circumstances in the various states.   The Republicans nationally placed first priority on the party's success in the state, not on which faction controlled the party; they believed that for Wisconsin, Senator La Follette was the best man to assure the widest possible Republican success.

Robert M. La Follette, Jr. had become something of a symbol of respectability, an accolade his father never received. His manner was quiet, his demeanor proper and courteous, and he was devoted to his duties in the Senate. He never became the storm-center of violent controversy as his father had been. "Robert La Follette has been a progressive, industrious, and useful Senator," *The New York Times* said editorially.[89] He is a "hard-working, able, and outstanding senator," Harold Ickes said in a radio speech, and his defeat "would be a national loss."[90] Leo T. Crowley, for years Wisconsin's leading Democrat in the Roosevelt administration, endorsed Senator La Follette and urged his Democratic friends to vote for him; "every liberal in Wisconsin should support him in a non-partisan manner."[91] Senator La Follette had acquired a reputation for honesty, integrity, and ability; he had become a "Senator's Senator" with the respect of his colleagues and the press. "I consider Sen. La Follette as one of the most honest and most able men in the senate, and have for years," C. P. Trussell of *The New York Times* said. "That is pretty much the view of all the boys in the [press] gallery."[92] Robert M. La Follette, Jr. was, at fifty-one, an elder statesman, an able and efficient and trustworthy civil service Senator.

The 1946 campaign in Wisconsin seemed dull and listless. This was the first election held in peace time since 1938. After the intense activity and extensive demands of the war years, years when imminent disaster hung over the heads of the American people, the relief of peace was so great that a mere political campaign could not arouse voter interest. The immediate aftermath of a total war bred political indifference. But the 1946 Wisconsin primary campaign was singularly listless. There were no major contests in the Democratic primary. In the Republican primary a popular Governor and a popular Senator both faced challenges which seemed unworthy of notice. John Wyngaard, a pro-Coleman correspondent, reported that "there is an unnatural apathy and pessimism in important sectors of the Republican party organism, stalwart wing, of Wisconsin."[93] The Republican organization sensed that defeat was its destiny. "The current indications are that the long reign of the La Follette dynasty in this state suffers no serious danger of interruption," a *New York Times* correspondent said.[94] Public interest was low because, with the end

of the war people were in no mood for politics, and because
there was no dramatic contest to arouse their interest.

Senator Robert M. La Follette, Jr. returned to Washington
immediately after the Portage Convention, and there he remained until Congress adjourned in the first days of August.
In the exuberance of the 1940 victory, Aldric Revell had said
that, in 1946, La Follette's "opponent, whoever he is, will
have small chance of defeating him."[95] This feeling persisted
among La Follette's supporters and most political observers.
On April 1, 1946, La Follette made the formal announcement of
his candidacy, amidst the widespread belief that he would win
with ease. He believed that he had been a good Senator, and
he was proud of his record:

> My platform is my record. My campaign will be
> based on my 20 years service to the people of Wis-
> consin and my fight for the liberal principals [*sic*]
> which the Progressive movement has pioneered. I
> invite the voters of Wisconsin to a consideration
> of those principles and my record in carrying them
> out. . . .
>
> In my campaign, I intend to discuss the critical
> issues of our time with the people of Wisconsin. I
> shall use every opportunity to do so which does not
> interfere with my duties in the U.S. Senate.[96]

Ideally, a Senator must combine the function of being a
legislator, of drafting laws for the general welfare of the nation, with the task of being a politician, of tending to political matters in his home state. In his first fifteen years in the
Senate, La Follette had played his role as a politician with
some enthusiasm and with considerable skill. During the war
he displayed less enthusiasm for his state political duties
than he had before; by 1946 he preferred his role as a legislator almost to the exclusion of his role as a state politician.
He expressed misgivings about the upciming election in late
1945 and early 1946 because he did not want to give in to the
demands of a strenuous political campaign.[97]   Despite his
growing distaste for political activity, his present job had an
understandable appeal to him; since he was twenty-four, he
had worked in the Senate. Senator La Follette wanted to be

re-elected because he was a statesman who had built a record deserving support, not because he was a state politician who could conduct a winning campaign. He had not only grown to detest campaigning; he hoped that he had risen to the point where, for his own political success, it was unnecessary.

On May 19, Senator La Follette opened his campaign with a radio speech from Washington. Because of the "vital and far-reaching" issues before Congress, La Follette told his supporters, "I shall have to rely on your radio and a long distance hook-up to bring us together."[98] His speech revealed an unabashed pride in his record:

> With 20 years of service spelling out in detail on the public record, I think you have an ample basis for making an appraisal of my candidacy—without numerous political speeches on my part. . . .
> I am running on my record. All the evidence is there for you to read, discuss, debate, and decide. . . . I merely want to say that I have worked hard at my job. I believe I can say, without boasting, that I have mastered the techniques of government, which have become extremely complicated. . . .

He then touched on foreign affairs, saying that it was not enough just to join international organizations, but that if the United States is to play a positive role in shaping peace it must strike at the causes of war itself.[99] Throughout the rest of May and through June and July, La Follette relied only on weekly radio speeches to reach Wisconsin. As usual, La Follette did not mention the other candidates by name, and he referred only indirectly to his opponent when he said that "the huge money bags have been opened up by the opposition in this campaign. . . . But the rank and file are not fooled by these tactics."[100] Senator La Follette's campaign stuck mainly to domestic issues—minimum wages, liberalized social security, expanded rural electrification—and largely ignored foreign affairs. Until Congress adjourned, until the last week of the campaign, Senator La Follette's weekly radio speeches from Washington were his only direct contact with Wisconsin.

Senator La Follette probably would have remained in Washington during the summer under any circumstances, but his

presence was assured because the La Follette-Monroney Congressional Reorganization bill was before Congress. La Follette's colleagues regarded him as one of the best men in the
Senate; yet, though they respected him as a statesman who
shaped policy, they valued him even more as a craftsman who
understood the mechanism which determines policy. He was
a skilled parliamentarian, but he was disturbed that the American legislative system did not function more smoothly. Since
1925, when he first entered the Senate, La Follette had seen
the Senator's task become increasingly complex. The growing
role of the federal government in the economic and social life
of the nation, and the greatly expanded federal budgets, had
produced far more bills for each Congressman to consider.
Pressure groups from all sides had not diminished in influence;
with the new role of organized labor they were more powerful
than ever before. Finally, the committee structure struck La
Follette as the height of legislative illogic. The committees
were not organized according to any rational plan. In the past,
whenever a new problem arose a new committee sprang to life.
Committees had accumulated like old magazines.

In 1943 Senator Francis T. Maloney of Connecticut and
Representative A. S. Mike Monroney of Oklahoma, with La Follette's enthusiastic support, introduced a resolution to form a
joint Senate-House committee to study and to make recommendations on the problem of congressional reorganization. In
January, 1945, Senator Maloney died, and Senator La Follette
became chairman of the Joint Committee on the Organization
of Congress. It was a rare tribute, for La Follette was not a
member of the Democratic majority. On March 4, 1946, two
weeks before the Portage Convention, the committee presented
its recommendations, which contained three main provisions:
1) each Congressman would receive an administrative assistant and Congressional committees would be provided with
staffs of experts, 2) lobbyists would be required to register,
and 3) the number of standing committees would be reduced
from forty-eight to eighteen in the House and from thirty-three
to sixteen in the Senate. This proposal to reorganize the committees and reduce their number was, to La Follette, "the key-
stone of the arch of the whole plan."[101]

When Senator La Follette introduced the bill in Congress

on May 13, it was given little chance for passage.   In June the Senate approved the bill by a surprisingly wide margin. The Associated Press reported that La Follette "led the floor fight throughout the senate debate. . . . Only 24 hours ago, the measure was given little chance of getting anywhere but now has a chance of becoming law during this session of Congress."[102] The Senator remained in Washington to help insure its passage in the House. "I am firmly convinced," A. S. Mike Monroney said years later, "that it was the personal leadership and recognized ability of Bob La Follette that secured consideration of the bill by the Senate and the House and opened the way for its enactment into law."[103] The bill passed the House late in July, just a few days before Congressional adjournment.   "To push it through," *Life* magazine said editorially, "required a rare combination of high political seriousness and parliamentary skill. La Follette has both."[104]

Eleven days before the primary in Wisconsin, President Truman signed the La Follette-Monroney Reorganization Act. La Follette probably considered this law his crowning achievement as a Senator. The provisions granting administrative assistants for all Congressmen and staffs of experts for the various committees were undoubtedly beneficial, but the law as a whole probably was not as crucial or as important as La Follette believed it to be.   The number of standing committees was reduced by more than half, but within a few years subcommittees had multiplied like rabbits.   Perhaps inefficiency was so ingrained in Congress that no tinkering with the machinery would have any substantial effect. Certainly the Reorganization Act did not give La Follette a dramatic or a colorful campaign issue.

There were other important measures before Congress—a minimum wage bill, price controls, and the problem of demobilization and the adaptation from a war-time to a peace-time economy—but to La Follette none mattered as much as his Reorganization bill.   Outside of his weekly radio speeches, he did virtually nothing about the primary campaign.   Senator George Aiken, a personal friend, expressed his apprehension at the situation in Wisconsin, and later recalled: "I had heard disturbing rumors from Wisconsin, and in the early part of July I spoke to Bob and told him that he ought to go home, for his

own good, to assure his nomination. He expressed himself as
being apprehensive about it and felt that probably he would
not be re-nominated, but he said he could not go home because
he had to look after his bill."[105]   In the middle of July, Aldric
Revell traveled to Washington to write some feature articles
on the Senator for *The Capital Times*, which was vigorously
supporting his candidacy.   One day at lunch La Follette told
Revell that he thought he was losing.   These words surprised
Revell,[106] as well they would have surprised most La Follette
supporters.   Robert M. La Follette, Jr. was a moody, easily
depressed man; he might have used these pessimistic words
to make the blow of defeat easier for himself and his supporters were it to come.   Yet, no matter how often he said
he might lose, Senator La Follette had substantial reasons for
expecting to win.   He heard repeated assurances from his
friends in Wisconsin that all was well. The conservative John
Wyngaard wrote just after the primary that "practically every
professional political observer" thought that La Follette would
win.[107]   Some polls reportedly showed him ahead by a three-
to-one margin.[108]   One political correspondent wrote that reports coming to Senator La Follette in June indicated that he
was stronger than he was six years before, when he had won
by a slender margin.[109]   Wherever he turned, La Follette saw
himself cast as the heavy favorite.

Congress finally adjourned in the early days of August.
In 1942 and 1944 Senator La Follette had contributed a week
of campaigning for the Progressive ticket. Now, when his own
future was at stake, he still campaigned for only a week.   La
Follette clearly was acting "as if he didn't like to campaign,"
Ralph Immell later recalled.[110]   "Bob didn't care if he was re-
elected or not," Glenn Roberts has said.[111] His campaign was
too short to do him much good, but it did give him just enough
time to make what turned out to be a fatal blunder. Ironically,
if he had not campaigned at all, if he had not made this mistake, he might have won the nomination with no campaign
whatsoever. In his speeches, La Follette repeated the themes
and the issues that he had told the voters over the radio.   He
also said that in this campaign there is "a technique of smear
and confusion—a streamlined version of mud-slinging.   It's
really not new or novel.   The Communists in this country and

in Russia rely on tactics of this kind to achieve and maintain devious objectives."[112]

"As the present campaign opens up in this state all eyes are being turned to the contest for governor," Miles McMillin wrote. "Ordinarily the U.S. senate race would attract more attention than it has, but there is a definite sentiment that no challenge worthy of note has been raised to Sen. Robert M. La Follette's re-election."[113] The La Follette supporters were split in the gubernatorial race between General Immell and Governor Goodland. General Immell had been closely associated with the La Follettes for more than two decades. In the past three years, Governor Goodland had built a reservoir of good will among the Progressives. The Progressives were lining up behind Goodland before Immell entered the race, but when Immell became a candidate the Progressives were split between the two men. La Follette said nothing about the contest for Governor. Goodland and Immell remained silent on the Senate race. "I am furthering no candidacy other than my own," the Governor said.[114] Because his supporters were split on the race for Governor, La Follette's best course lay in benevolent neutrality.

Earlier in the campaign, La Follette had shown an "apparent determination" to keep out of the gubernatorial race.[115] Nevertheless, the Immell supporters felt that La Follette could provide an invaluable assist to the General's campaign; they wanted the Senator to give him a public endorsement. Phil La Follette told Immell that his brother should endorse him.[116] Bob was uncertain as to how he should respond to this pressure. "As long as Mr. La Follette was in Milwaukee County I was able to keep him from making that type of endorsement," the Executive Director of the La Follette for Senator Club in Milwaukee has recalled.[117] Francis H. Wendt, a Progressive Republican and a former Mayor of Racine, said that "all liberal Republicans were supporting Governor Goodland and Senator La Follette for re-election." La Follette "asked my advice as to whether he ought to" endorse Immell. "It was my own opinion that he should not do it."[118] One of the leaders of a group supporting both La Follette and Goodland has recalled that "Senator La Follette had pledged himself to this group not to endorse General Immell during the campaign. He repeated that many times, and we carried his assurance back to Governor Goodland who was most pleased with it, and told us he would not endorse McCarthy."[119]

The Immell camp tried to assure La Follette that he was in no danger, that he could not possibly jeopardize his own position, that he should endorse Immell as repayment for years of loyal service to the cause of Progressivism. In Racine, five days before the primary, Senator La Follette did just that. "I have lots of respect for Gov. Goodland," La Follette said. "However, I have known Ralph Immell for 25 years. . . . I personally am going to vote for Immell."[120] Immell thanked La Follette, and in turn he endorsed the Senator. Years later, Immell said that he had not endorsed La Follette earlier for he did not want to appear to be begging for support in return.[121]

La Follette's endorsement of Immell shattered the neutrality that the Goodland and La Follette supporters had expected from each other. La Follette's action "came as a blow, and a shock, to those of us who were supporting both" La Follette and Goodland, and "disrupted the unity of the organization" supporting both candidates.[122] According to the director of La Follette's campaign in Milwaukee, La Follette's endorsement of Immell "definitely killed his chances for re-election because Governor Goodland's supporters on the night of the endorsement, as I am reliably informed, sent out over ten thousand telegrams alienating any support which they may have been giving to Mr. La Follette and were ordered to support Mr. McCarthy."[123] Chairman Coleman promptly switched the support of the Republican organization to Goodland. The original organization candidate, Delbert J. Kenny, did not stand a chance, and Coleman now had to prevent an Immell victory, which would represent a La Follette victory.[124] Because La Follette had come out against Goodland, Coleman could safely support the Governor. The chairman's action brought many Goodland partisans who would have voted for La Follette to McCarthy's banner. La Follette's endorsement of Immell did the Senator undeniable harm.

Nevertheless, the campaign came to a close with La Follette still heavily favored to win. James Reston, covering the campaign for *The New York Times*, wrote that "Senator Robert M. La Follette is expected to prove tomorrow in the Wisconsin primary election that a man can bolt the Republican party and get away with it."[125] Senator La Follette concluded his brief campaign with a radio speech, in which he said: "I am proud of the enemies I have made. I am proud that the little group that sits in Communist headquarters in Milwaukee and the tight little corporation that sits in Coleman headquarters in the Lorraine hotel here in Madison have chosen me to be the target of their venemous [*sic*] attacks, their fradulent propaganda, and their neurotic editorials."[126]

Primary day was Tuesday, August 13, 1946. As expected, there was a very light turnout; fewer than 500,000 voters went to the polls. The first returns established the trend that would continue for several hours—a neck and neck race between Senator La Follette and Judge McCarthy, with the Senator holding a slim lead in the rural areas which reported first. Jack K. Kyle saw the portent of the outcome in the results of Adams County, always one of the first to report and always a La Follette stronghold. Yet, this time, La Follette's margin in Adams County was dangerously thin.[127] Milwaukee County was one of the last to report, and it provided the decisive margin, as it did in 1940. In that year Fred H. Clausen actually ran ahead of La Follette by 2,903 votes outside of Milwaukee County; La Follette's plurality of 54,820 in Milwaukee provided his margin of victory.[128] In 1946, Senator La Follette rolled up a lead of 4,781 votes in Wisconsin's seventy other counties, but Milwaukee handed the young judge a plurality of 10,159 votes, more than enough to wipe out La Follette's outstate lead. Judge McCarthy won, 207,935 to 202,557 votes.[129] Senator La Follette conceded defeat to McCarthy in a one-word telegram, saying simply "Congratulations." Though he was happy to see Governor Goodland defeat Immell by a somewhat wider margin, Thomas E. Coleman received his greatest joy from La Follette's defeat; he has said repeatedly that this was the greatest night in his life.[130]

An analysis of the vote shows that La Follette held the traditional Progressive strongholds in the rural northwestern part of the state, and even increased his strength there from what it had been in 1940. The most significant vote, however, came from the industrial and labor area in the southwestern part of the state, mainly Kenosha, Racine, and Milwaukee

Counties.   Senator La Follette had carried all three counties impressively in 1934 and again in 1940.   In 1946, however, he lost all three counties.   McCarthy took Kenosha, 3,576 to 3,410 votes, Racine by a margin of 5,569 to 4,370, and Milwaukee with a vote of 48,596 to La Follette's 38,437. Howard J. McMurray ran unopposed for the Democratic nomination. In Kenosha, he received 4,044 votes, more than either La Follette or McCarthy, in Racine he received 3,630 votes, and in Milwaukee he received 31,816 votes.   Whereas La Follette received only twenty-three per cent of his total vote and McCarthy received but twenty-eight per cent of his total vote in these three counties, McMurray received sixty-three per cent of his total primary vote in Kenosha, Racine, and Milwaukee.[131] Much of the labor vote failed to support Senator La Follette by entering the Democratic primary to support McMurray, and, in Milwaukee's Fourth Congressional District, to nominate Edmund Bobrowicz. This result, achieved in this way, was precisely what Democratic and labor leaders had hoped to accomplish.   The loss of labor support was the most important single factor in the defeat of Senator Robert M. La Follette, Jr.
    Before the primary, Senator La Follette claimed that the Communists in the Wisconsin C.I.O. had singled him out for attack because he had criticized the Soviet Union; he constantly referred to this in his campaign speeches.   An article in a national news magazine   in June, 1946, describing the Senator's work on the Reorganization bill, also mentioned in passing La Follette's campaign in Wisconsin, and said: "Senator La Follette thinks the present opposition [of labor] comes from extreme left-wing units within the unions, units that dislike his criticism of Russia."[132]   After his defeat La Follette talked with Marquis Childs, and Childs wrote: "La Follette believes his desertion by labor was the product of a deliberate campaign by the extreme left—under communist domination—to defeat him because of his stand on foreign policy.   He attributes the start of this campaign to criticism of Soviet Russia which he made in a speech in May of 1945."[133] La Follette had some justification for this belief.   Yet, the state C.I.O.'s major task was not, as La Follette believed, his defeat; its major objective was the success of Democratic candidates.   In supporting Democrats, which was its goal and

not the cover for a more sinister plot, organized labor hurt La Follette, for it siphoned into the Democratic primary voters who would have supported La Follette had they chosen to vote in the Republican primary.

In addition to the loss of labor support, many other factors contributed to La Follette's defeat. During the war years Senator La Follette had allowed his political machine to deteriorate, his political fences to fall; after the war, when presumably politics-as-normal could return, La Follette did not repair the damage to his own organization. His endorsement of General Immell proved to be a political blunder of the first magnitude, for it alienated many who would have supported him while giving his own candidacy no new strength; it makes sense only if La Follette believed that he could not fail to win the nomination. His week of campaigning hurt him in another way, for it was so short, such an obviously brief and hurried affair, it only went to underscore one charge which Coleman and McCarthy had repeatedly made against him, that he was "the Gentleman from Virginia" who did not give a tinker's dam about the common man of Wisconsin. As a Washington Senator he appeared too aloof, too remote from Wisconsin. "He has taken root in Washington," *The Washington Post* said a few years later, "and he relied on the Progressive tradition in Wisconsin to see him through."[134]

Joseph R. McCarthy probably would not have won without his vigorous and aggressive and energetic campaign. Yet, in the final analysis, his campaign could not have been successful if La Follette had not so thoroughly dissipated his own strength. The La Follette name was still formidable; despite the indifference and mistakes of his campaign, and McCarthy's unceasing efforts, the final vote was very close. Senator La Follette had relied on his name and the tradition and political strength it represented. In 1946, this was not enough. "I didn't go back to talk to the voters," he was quoted as saying. "My father did just what Joe McCarthy did [to win], and I guess I made a mistake."[135]

A *New York Times* correspondent reported that La Follette's defeat was "much to the surprise and sorrow of a large group of the Senate, who, while frequently disagreeing with him on matters of policy and ideology, highly respected his

honesty and integrity."[136] *Newsweek* also expressed regret
that La Follette had been defeated in words which, both in tone
and substance, would hardly have fit the elder La Follette:

> In the final analysis, the loss that La Follette sus-
> tained was shared by the Senate. Among his col-
> leagues, he was rated at the top. He was a legisla-
> tive craftsman in the British sense, molded by birth,
> breeding, and training to be a public servant. Few
> members of Congress, whether they agreed with him
> politically or not, failed to concede that La Follette
> possessed all the faculties necessary to make the
> parliamentary system work.[137]

After his defeat, Robert M. La Follette, Jr. drifted forever
from politics. In November, 1946, Second District Congressman Robert K. Henry died. Both Mrs. Philip F. La Follette and
Norman Clapp urged Bob to run for the vacant House seat. As
Clapp has remembered it, Bob replied: "If the people of Wis-
cinson would be content to let me come to Washington and
serve as a Congressman, I would be happy. But they won't let
me. They would make me go out and rebuild the Progressive
movement. I am not as young as I was. I don't have it in me."[138]
In retrospect, 1946 was a crucial year for the political
development of Wisconsin. The attempted Progressive invasion of the Republican party failed. Within a few years some
of the remnants of the Progressive party and many young Roosevelt Democrats completely captured the Democratic party. The
Republican party remained in the hands of the conservative
elements which had controlled it since 1934. The 1946 results merely consolidated the conservatives' control. With
each passing year Wisconsin was moving closer to a real two-
party rivalry and, in 1958, the Democrats elected a United
States Senator, a Governor, and gained control of the state
Assembly. In 1946, the most important result of the election
was the defeat of Robert Marion La Follette, Jr. For months,
even for years after August 13, 1946, Joseph R. McCarthy was
known to the nation primarily as "the man who beat La Follette." "In our day only the Roosevelt family, in both its
branches, has overshadowed it," *The New York Times* said
about the La Follettes on Young Bob's defeat. "Perhaps he,

too, recognizes it as the end of an era."[139] For forty-six years a La Follette had been either Governor of Wisconsin, or United States Senator, or both; in 1946 that came to an end. Wisconsin politics would never be quite the same again.

NOTES

CHAPTER I

1. Bruce Bliven, "Robert M. La Follette," *The New Republic*, Volume 43 (July 1, 1925), pp. 144—45.

2. *The New York Times*, June 23, 1925, p. 19.

3. Note written by Henry Allen Cooper at end of letter, E. G. Smith to Cooper, September 16, 1925, Cooper papers.

4. *The Capital Times*, August 28, 1924.

5. *Ibid.*, August 16, 1924.

6. Frederick William Wile, *The Capital Times*, July 22, 1925, p. 2.

7. *The New York Times*, June 19, 1925, p. 1.

8. *The Capital Times*, July 3, 1925, p. 1.

9. *Ibid.*, September 30, 1925, p. 1.

10. Robert S. Allen, *The Wisconsin State Journal*, April 12, 1925.

11. "'Young Bob,'" *The Nation*, Volume 121 (July 8, 1925), p. 59.

12. *The Capital Times*, July 30, 1925, p. 1.

13. Ralph Sucher to Frank Walsh, July 22, 1925, Cooper papers.

14. Robert M. La Follette, Jr. to "Dear Friend," August 20, 1925, clipping in Legislative Reference Service files, The Republican Party of Wisconsin.

15. John Mandt Nelson to Henry Allen Cooper, August 20, 1925, Cooper papers.

16. *The Capital Times*, August 17, 1925, p. 1.

17. Henry F. Pringle, "Youth at the Top," *World's Work*,

Volume 58 (May, 1929), p. 158.

18. Elmer Davis, "The Wisconsin Brothers," *Harpers*, Volume 178 (February, 1939), p. 271; Pringle, p. 158.

19. *The Capital Times*, August 25, 1925, p. 4.

20. *Ibid.*, August 31, 1925, p. 3.

21. *The New York Times*, July 27, 1925, p. 16.

22. *The Capital Times*, August 10, 1925, p. 4.

23. *Ibid.*, July 1, 1925, p. 1.

24. *Ibid.*, September 12, 1925, p. 3.

25. *Ibid.*, September 9, 1925, p. 4.

26. *Ibid.*, July 17, 1925, p. 2.

27. *Ibid.*, September 15, 1925, p. 11.

28. *Ibid.*, August 5, 1925, p. 2.

29. *Ibid.*, August 20, 1925, p. 14.

30. *Ibid.*, September 11, 1925, p. 1.

31. *The New York Times*, August 19, 1925, p. 2.

32. *The Capital Times*, August 7, 1925, p. 20.

33. *The Wisconsin Blue Book*, 1927, p. 500.

34. *The New York Times*, September 17, 1925, p. 22.

35. *Ibid.*, September 17, 1925, p. 1.

36. *The Capital Times*, September 17, 1925, p. 1.

37. *The New York Times*, September 20, 1925, IX, p. 5.

38. *Ibid.*, September 28, 1925, p. 10.

39. *The Capital Times*, August 24, 1925, p. 1.

40. *The New York Times*, September 18, 1925, p. 12.

41. *The Capital Times*, September 18, 1925, p. 1.

42. *Ibid.*, September 24, 1925, p. 11.

43. *The Wisconsin Blue Book*, 1927, p. 579.

44. *The New York Times*, September 30, 1925, p. 1.

45. *Ibid.*, October 1, 1925, p. 29.

46. *The Capital Times*, September 30, 1925, p. 20.

47. Clarence E. Cason, "The La Follette Succession," *The Independent*, Volume 119 (July 2, 1927), p. 8.

48. *The New York Times*, October 1, 1925, p. 26.

49. *The Capital Times*, October 2, 1925, p. 3.

50. Frank R. Kent, "Little Bob Wins," *The Nation*, Volume 121 (December 30, 1925), p. 758.

51. Robert M. La Follette, Jr., "La Follette Progressivism in 1928," *Current History*, Volume 28 (June, 1928), pp. 357—59.

52. Ludwell Denny, Quoted in *Literary Digest*, Volume 97 (June 30, 1928), p. 40.

53. *The New York Times*, July 13, 1928, p. 4.

54. *Ibid.*, August 27, 1928, p. 18.

55. *The Wisconsin Blue Book*, 1929, pp. 735, 815—16.

56. Pringle, p. 156.

57. *The New York Times*, September 18, 1930, p. 26.

58. Mauritz A. Hallgren, "The New Radicalism in America," *Contemporary Review*, Volume 142 (July, 1932), pp. 56—57; see also, by the same author, "Young Bob La Follette," *The Nation*, Volume 132 (March 4, 1931), p. 235.

59. Elmer Davis, "Wisconsin is Different," *Harpers*, Volume 165 (October, 1932), p. 618.

60. Edward N. Doan, *The La Follettes and the Wisconsin Idea*, (New York, 1947), p. 150.

61. "Spy Profits," *Literary Digest*, Volume 123 (March 27, 1937), p. 56.

CHAPTER II

1. Fred C. Sheasby, *The New York Times*, February 3, 1929, III, p. 2.

2. *Ibid.*, December 8, 1929, III, p. 1.

3. Louis H. Cook, "Ruling Dynasty of Wisfollette," *The Saturday Evening Post*, Volume 203 (December 6, 1930), pp. 18—19.

4. S. T. Williamson, *The New York Times*, September 21, 1930, X, p. 2.

5. *The Wisconsin Blue Book*, 1933, p. 515.

6. Elmer Davis, "Wisconsin is Different," *Harpers*, Volume 165 (October, 1932), p. 614.

7. *The Wisconsin Blue Book*, 1933, pp. 531, 533.

8. Interview with Ralph M. Immell, January 31, 1962.

9. Thomas R. Amlie to Warren J. Sawall, April 22, 1961, Amlie papers.

10. *Ibid.*

11. *Ibid.*

12. Charles C. Holmburg, *The Capital Times*, February

25, 1934, p. 1.

13. Fred Sheasby, *The New York Times*, August 2, 1931, III, p. 5.

14. Thomas R. Amlie to Warren J. Sawall, April 22, 1961, Amlie papers.

15. Paul H. Douglas, "State Farmer-Labor Parties," *World Tomorrow*, Volume 16 (September 28, 1933), p. 544.

16. Mark Rhea Byers, "A New La Follette Party," *North American Review*, Volume 237 (May, 1934), p. 407.

17. Interview with Philip F. La Follette, July 24, 1961.

18. *The Capital Times*, September 30, 1925, p. 1.

19. *The New York Times*, March 7, 1931, p. 20.

20. Robert M. La Follette, Jr. to Philip F. La Follette, October 18, 1933, Philip F. La Follette papers.

21. Robert M. La Follette, Jr. to Philip F. La Follette, February 16, 1934, Philip F. La Follette papers.

22. *The Capital Times*, February 25, 1934, p. 1.

23. Interview with Norman M. Clapp, August 2, 1961.

24. *The Capital Times*, March 3, 1934, p. 1; *Ibid.*, March 4, 1934, p. 1; Byers, p. 406.

25. Byers, p. 408.

26. State of Wisconsin, In Supreme Court, January Term, 1934, Herman L. Ekern, et al. vs. Theodore Dammann, Brief of Plaintiffs, pp. 2—3.

27. Jacque and Lorraine Hopkins, "Wisconsin's Conscience: William T. Evjue," *The Nation*, Volume 181 (November 12, 1955), pp. 419—20.

28. Robert M. La Follette, Jr., Speech to the Fond du Lac Convention, May 19, 1934, State Historical Society of Wisconsin.

29. La Follette interview.

30. S. J. Duncan-Clark, *The New York Times*, August 5, 1934, IV, p. 1.

31. "Progressive State Platform," *The Wisconsin Blue Book*, 1935, pp. 476—77.

32. Wallace S. Sayre, "Left Turn in Wisconsin," *The New Republic*, Volume 80 (October 24, 1934), pp. 300—2.

33. *The New York Times*, August 13, 1934, p. 4.

34. *Ibid.*, August 17, 1934, p. 11.

35. *Ibid.*, October 20, 1934, p. 2.

36. Robert M. La Follette, Jr. to Philip F. La Follette, June 4, 1934, Philip F. La Follette papers.

37. Press Conference No. 133, June 27, 1934, quoted in James MacGregor Burns, *Roosevelt: The Lion and the Fox,* (New York, 1956), p. 201.

38. *The New York Times,* August 10, 1934, p. 1.

39. *Ibid.,* September 20, 1934, p. 22.

40. S. J. Duncan-Clark, *The New York Times,* September 16, 1934, IV, p. 7.

41. *The Wisconsin Blue Book,* 1935, pp. 613, 618.

42. *The New York Times,* October 23, 1934, p. 16.

43. *Ibid.,* July 28, 1935, II, p. 3.

44. *Ibid.,* November 9, 1934, p. 2.

45. *Ibid.,* September 29, 1936, p. 23.

46. *Ibid.,* May 20, 1937, p. 2.

47. Interview with Thomas R. Amlie, May 4, 1961; Immell interview.

48. Philip F. La Follette, "A New Movement. . .The National Progressives of America . . . Is Under Way," Speech delivered on April 28, 1938, copy at the State Historical Society of Wisconsin. See also, "The Party of Our Time: The National Progressives Organize," *Vital Speeches of the Day,* Volume 4 (May 5, 1938), pp. 450–55, for another copy of the same speech.

49. Burns, p. 358.

50. *The New York Times,* January 3, 1937, VIII, p. 9.

51. *Ibid.,* April 25, 1938, p. 7.

52. *Ibid.,* April 26, 1938, p. 4.

53. *Ibid.,* April 28, 1938, p. 1.

54. Quoted in "La Follettes' Third Party Flag Flaps in Political Cross Winds," *Newsweek,* Volume II (May 9, 1938), p. 10.

55. Robert M. La Follette, Jr., Speech for the National Progressives of America, May 9, 1938, State Historical Society of Wisconsin.

56. Clapp interview.

57. La Follette interview.

58. Miles McMillin, "Wisconsin—Anybody's Guess," *The Nation,* Volume 166 (April 3, 1948), p. 374.

59. Interview with Morris Rubin, May 4, 1961; Interview with Aldric Revell, July 15, 1961; Interview with William T.

Evjue, July 18, 1961; Amlie interview; Clapp interview.

60. *The New York Times*, March 23, 1935, p. 12.

61. Arthur M. Schlesinger, Jr., *The Politics of Upheaval*, (Boston, 1960), p. 136.

62. Robert E. Sherwood, *Roosevelt and Hopkins*, (New York, 1950), pp. 94—95.

63. "Progressives at Madison," *Time*, Volume 31 (May 9, 1938), p. 11.

64. Robert M. La Follette, Jr., speech of May 9, 1938.

65. *The New York Times*, August 26, 1938, p. 16.

66. Aldric Revell, *The New York Times*, April 23, 1939, IV, p. 10.

67. Paul Y. Anderson, "La Follette's Bid for Power," *The Nation*, Volume 146 (May 7, 1938), pp. 524—25.

68. Leon D. Epstein, *Politics in Wisconsin*, (Madison, 1958), p. 43.

69. *The Wisconsin Blue Book*, 1940, p. 606.

70. Thomas R. Amlie to Warren J. Sawall, April 22, 1961, Amlie papers.

71. Amlie interview; Evjue interview.

72. Elmer Davis, "The Wisconsin Brothers," *Harpers*, Volume 178 (February, 1939), p. 269.

73. Oswald Garrison Villard, "Pillars of Government: Robert M. La Follette, Jr.," *Forum & Century*, Volume 96 (August, 1936), p. 89.

74. Delbert Clark, "Who Will it Be in 1940? The Guessing Starts," *The New York Times Magazine*, November 21, 1937, p. 3.

75. Robert M. La Follette, Jr., "The Neutrality Issue," *Vital Speeches of the Day*, Volume 6 (November 1, 1939), pp. 59—60.

CHAPTER III

1. *The New York Times*, December 22, 1939, p. 1.

2. Interview with Thomas R. Amlie, May 4, 1961.

3. Gustave J. Keller to Orland Loomis, October 25, 1940, Loomis papers.

4. Charles H. Backstrom, "The Progressive Party of Wis-

consin, 1934—1946," Unpublished Ph.D. Dissertation, University of Wisconsin, 1956, p. 314.

   5. *The Milwaukee Journal*, October 3, 1940, II, p. 5.
   6. Interview with Norman M. Clapp, August 2, 1961.
   7. Interview with William R. Voigt, May 5, 1961.
   8. Interview with Jack K. Kyle, May 8, 1961.
   9. Robert M. La Follette, Jr. to "Dear Friend," September 3, 1940, Loomis papers.
   10. *The Capital Times*, May 13, 1940, p. 19.
   11. *Ibid.*, May 19, 1940, p. 1.
   12. *Ibid.*, May 20, 1940, p. 4.
   13. Aldric Revell, *The Capital Times*, May 7, 1940, p. 5.
   14. *The Sheboygan Press*, September 7, 1940, p. 3.
   15. *The Capital Times* , September 15, 1925, p. 1.
   16. Fred C. Sheasby, *The New York Times*, March 15, 1936, IV, p. 11.
   17. Elmer Davis, "The Wisconsin Brothers," *Harpers*, Volume 178 (February, 1939), p. 273.
   18. *The New York Times*, January 8, 1937, p. 1.
   19. *Ibid.*, November 10, 1938, p. 20.
   20. *The Milwaukee Journal*, September 12, 1940, p. 8.
   21. *The Sheboygan Press*, September 10, 1940, p. 5.
   22. *The Milwaukee Journal*, September 14, 1940, p. 10.
   23. *The Sheboygan Press*, September 13, 1940, p. 5.
   24. *The Milwaukee Journal* , September 12, 1940, p. 8.
   25. *The Sheboygan Press*, September 11, 1940, p. 8.
   26. *The Capital Times*, September 16, 1940, p. 6.
   27. Quoted in *ibid.*, September 18, 1940, p. 26.
   28. Quoted in *ibid.*
   29. *The Wisconsin Blue Book*, 1942, p. 583.
   30. Interview with Mr. and Mrs. Philip F. La Follette, July 24, 1961.
   31. *The Milwaukee Journal*, September 18, 1940, p. 12.
   32. Harold E. Stafford to "Dear Friend," August 22, 1940, Loomis papers.
   33. *The Sheboygan Press*, September 30, 1940, p. 1.
   34. *Ibid.*, October 2, 1940, p. 6.
   35. *The Milwaukee Journal*, October 10, 1940, p. 11.
   36. *Ibid.*, October 2, 1940, p. 11.
   37. *Ibid.*, October 4, 1940, p. 4.

38. *Ibid.*, October 17, 1940, p. 8.

39. *The Sheboygan Press*, October 22, 1940, p. 3.

40. *Ibid.*, October 2, 1940, p. 6.

41. *The Milwaukee Journal*, October 2, 1940, p. 11.

42. *Ibid.*, November 1, 1940, p. 13.

43. Raymond Clapper, "Nation at Large," *The Sheboygan Press*, October 22, 1940, p. 20.

44. *The Milwaukee Journal*, October 16, 1940, p. 15.

45. *The Sheboygan Press*, September 30, 1940, p. 7.

46. *Ibid.*, October 3, 1940, p. 9.

47. *Ibid.*, September 30, 1940, p. 7.

48. *The Milwaukee Journal*, October 3, 1940, p. 9.

49. *The Sheboygan Press*, October 22, 1940, p. 3.

50. *The Milwaukee Journal*, September 12, 1940, p. 21.

51. *The Sheboygan Press*, November 1, 1940, p. 4.

52. *The Milwaukee Journal*, September 12, 1940, p. 21.

53. *The Sheboygan Press*, October 11, 1940, p. 9.

54. *The Milwaukee Journal*, October 15, 1940, p. 6.

55. *The Sheboygan Press*, September 3, 1940, p. 10.

56. Fred Sheasby, *The Milwaukee Journal*, October 27, 1940, p. 15.

57. *The Sheboygan Press*, October 3, 1940, p. 9.

58. *The Milwaukee Journal*, October 23, 1940, p. 19.

59. *Ibid.*, October 27, 1940, p. 14.

60. *Ibid.*, October 25, 1940, p. 18.

61. *Ibid.*, October 21, 1940, II, p. 8.

62. *The Capital Times*, September 12, 1940, p. 10.

63. Voigt interview.

64. *The New York Times*, February 1, 1928, p. 12.

65. *Ibid.*, July 8, 1927, p. 4.

66. From a Senate speech, February 7, 1928, quoted in *Congressional Digest*, Volume 7 (April, 1928), pp. 124—27.

67. *The Sheboygan Press*, September 30, 1940, p. 1.

68. *The New York Times*, October 1, 1940, p. 15.

69. Clapp interview.

70. *The Milwaukee Journal*, October 6, 1940, p. 14.

71. *The Sheboygan Press*, November 5, 1940, p. 10.

72. *The Milwaukee Journal*, October 1, 1940, p. 12.

73. *The Sheboygan Press*, October 4, 1940, p. 12

74. *The Milwaukee Journal*, October 12, 1940, p. 8.

75. *Ibid.*, October 18, 1940, p. 14.

76. *Ibid.*, October 20, 1940, p. 1.

77. *Ibid.*, October 21, 1940, p. 11.

78. *Ibid.*, October 23, 1940, p. 1.

79. *The New York Times*, October 23, 1940, p. 21.

80. *The Sheboygan Press*, November 2, 1940, p. 21.

81. John Burnham to Orland Loomis, October 2, 1940, Loomis papers.

82. Maurice B. Pasch to John Becker, October 30, 1940, Loomis papers.

83. *The New York Times*, October 28, 1940, p. 8.

84. *The Milwaukee Journal*, October 23, 1940, p. 14.

85. *The Wisconsin CIO News*, November 11, 1940, p. 3.

86. *The Milwaukee Journal*, October 23, 1940, p. 19.

87. *The Capital Times*, May 20, 1940, p. 1.

88. *The Milwaukee Journal*, November 4, 1940, p. 1.

89. Fred Sheasby, *The Milwaukee Journal*, September 29, 1940, p. 16.

90. J. C. Ralston, *The Milwaukee Journal*, September 22, 1940, p. 8.

91. Raymond Clapper, "Nation at Large," *The Sheboygan Press*, October 22, 1940, p. 20.

92. Drew Pearson and Robert S. Allen, "Washington Merry-Go-Round," *The Sheboygan Press*, October 31, 1940, p. 10.

93. *The Milwaukee Journal*, November 4, 1940, p. 12.

94. Clapp interview.

95. *The Milwaukee Journal*, November 4, 1940, p. 10.

96. *Ibid.*, November 5, 1940, p. 7.

97. Clapp interview.

98. *The Milwaukee Journal*, November 6, 1940, p. 1.

99. *The Wisconsin Blue Book*, 1942, pp. 654—61.

100. Aldric Revell, *The Capital Times*, November 10, 1940, p. 3.

101. Harold E. Stafford to "Dear Friend," August 22, 1940, Loomis papers.

102. Orland S. Loomis to Miss Grace Lynch, December 12, 1940, Loomis papers.

103. Otto F. Christenson to Orland S. Loomis, November 6, 1940, Loomis papers.

104. *The Sheboygan Press*, November 7, 1940, p. 36.

CHAPTER IV

1. *The Capital Times*, September 20, 1941, p. 1.
2. *Congressional Record*, October 29, 1941, 77:8325.
3. *The Capital Times*, October 16, 1941, p. 1.
4. Quoted in Arthur M. Schlesinger, Jr., *The Politics of Upheaval*, (Boston, 1960), p. 145.
5. *The Capital Times*, July 28, 1941, p. 1.
6. Quoted in *ibid.*, July 23, 1941, p. 3.
7. *Ibid.*, July 25, 1941, p. 1.
8. Winter Everett, *The Wisconsin State Journal*, July 25, 1941, p. 6.
9. *The Capital Times*, August 9, 1941, p. 1.
10. *Ibid.*, August 12, 1941, p. 1.
11. Interview with Philip E. La Follette, July 24, 1961.
12. Interview with Thomas R. Amlie, May 4, 1961.
13. *The Capital Times*, November 2, 1941, p. 1.
14. *The Milwaukee Journal*, September 12, 1940, p. 21.
15. *The Capital Times*, December 19, 1941, p. 1.
16. *Ibid.*, June 21, 1942, p. 1.
17. *Ibid.*, December 1, 1941, p. 1.
18. Thomas R. Amlie's reply to questionnaire to Warren J. Sawall, 1961, Amlie papers.
19. *The Capital Times*, June 15, 1942, p. 18.
20. John P. Varda to Orland S. Loomis, February 23, 1942, Loomis papers.
21. *The Capital Times*, February 25, 1942, p. 18.
22. Robert M. La Follette, Jr. to Philip F. La Follette, March 9, 1942, Philip F. La Follette papers.
23. La Follette interview.
24. Orland S. Loomis to Walter J. Rush, November 20, 1940, Loomis papers.
25. Interview with Maurice B. Pasch, June 8, 1961.
26. Orland S. Loomis to Lyall T. Beggs, May 21, 1941, Loomis papers.
27. *The Capital Times*, July 28, 1941, p. 1.
28. Interview with Norman M. Clapp, August 2, 1961.
29. *The Capital Times*, April 8, 1942, p. 1.
30. *Ibid.*, April 12, 1942, p. 1.
31. Robert H. North to Orland S. Loomis, May 29, 1942,

Loomis papers.

32. *The Capital Times*, August 8, 1942, p. 3.

33. *Ibid.*, June 30, 1942, p. 12.

34. Robert M. La Follette, Jr. to Orland S. Loomis, May 5, 1942, Loomis papers.

35. Interview with William R. Voigt, May 5, 1961.

36. Interview with Jack K. Kyle, May 8, 1961; Amlie interview.

37. Interview with Mrs. Philip F. La Follette, July 24, 1961.

38. *The Capital Times*, July 1, 1942, p. 8.

39. *Ibid.*, October 29, 1942, p. 6.

40. For a review of some of the more humorous aspects of Heil's Governorship see Harvey W. Schwandner, "Wisconsin's Problem Governor," *American Mercury*, Volume 48 (November, 1939), pp. 272—75.

41. *The Capital Times*, October 25, 1942, p. 5.

42. *Ibid.*, November 1, 1942, p. 4.

43. *Ibid.*, November 2, 1942, p. 4.

44. Orland S. Loomis to Roland Klaus, November 7, 1940, Loomis papers.

45. *The Wisconsin Blue Book*, 1944, pp. 572—76.

46. *The Wisconsin State Journal*, November 4, 1942, p. 6.

47. *The Capital Times*, November 5, 1942, p. 1.

48. *Ibid.*, December 8, 1942, p. 1.

49. Interview with Glenn D. Roberts, June 6, 1961; Kyle interview; Pasch interview; *The Capital Times*, November 1, 1945, p. 1; *The Milwaukee Journal*, November 20, 1945, II, p. 1.

50. *The Capital Times*, April 25, 1943, p. 28.

51. *Ibid.*, July 15, 1943, p. 1.

52. *Ibid.*, April 28, 1943, p. 2.

53. Robert M. La Follette, Jr. to Philip F. La Follette, June 24, 1943, Philip F. La Follette papers.

54. *The Capital Times*, August 15, 1943, p. 1.

55. *Ibid.*, May 7, 1944, p. 1.

56. *Ibid.*, April 18, 1945, p. 3.

57. *Ibid.*, August 29, 1944, p. 4.

58. *Ibid.*, August 21, 1944, p. 5.

59. *Ibid.*, October 23, 1944, p. 5.

60. *Ibid.*, October 16, 1944, p. 2.
61. *Ibid.*, October 20, 1944, p. 5.
62. *Ibid.*, November 2, 1944, p. 17.
63. *The Wisconsin Blue Book*, 1946, pp. 664—69.

CHAPTER V

1. *The Capital Times*, November 9, 1944, p. 9.
2. *Ibid.*, April 28, 1943, p. 2.
3. *Ibid.*, November 19, 1945, p. 3.
4. Alfred Bowman (pseudonym), "The Man Behind Mc-Carthy—Coleman of Wisconsin," *The Nation*, Volume 178 (March 20, 1954), pp. 236—37.
5. Aldric Revell, *The Capital Times*, October 28, 1945, p. 1.
6. Rex Karney, *The Wisconsin State Journal*, January 30, 1946, p. 4.
7. *The Capital Times*, November 17, 1944, p. 1.
8. *Ibid.*, January 31, 1945, p. 1.
9. *Ibid.*
10. *Ibid.*, February 20, 1945, p. 5.
11. *Ibid.*, March 21, 1945, p. 1.
12. *The Wisconsin CIO News*, February 19, 1945, p. 1.
13. *The Capital Times*, June 11, 1945, p. 2.
14. *Ibid.*, June 9, 1945, p. 1.
15. *Ibid.*, October 11, 1945, p. 1.
16. *Ibid.*, November 13, 1945, p. 1.
17. *Ibid.*, November 16, 1945, p. 1.
18. *Ibid.*, November 20, 1945, p. 18.
19. *Ibid.*, November 27, 1945, p. 3.
20. *The Milwaukee Journal*, November 20, 1945, II, p. 1.
21. *The Capital Times*, November 10, 1944, p. 1.
22. Quoted in Richard L. Neuberger, "Wisconsin's Tough Old Man," *The Saturday Evening Post*, Volume 218 (February 16, 1946), pp. 9—11.
23. *The Capital Times*, July 19, 1945, p. 22.
24. Miles McMillin, "Exit the Wisconsin Progressives," *The Nation*, Volume 162 (March 30, 1946), p. 367.

25. Interview with Ralph M. Immell, January 31, 1962.

26. *The Capital Times*, March 15, 1946, p. 1.

27. Immell interview.

28. *The Capital Times*, November 10, 1945, p. 1.

29. *Ibid.*, November 11, 1945, p. 1.

30. Howard J. McMurray to author, July 5, 1961.

31. *The Capital Times*, March 14, 1946, p. 1.

32. *Ibid.*, January 28, 1946, p. 5.

33. *The Sheboygan Press*, January 28, 1946, p. 16.

34. *Ibid.*, November 7, 1940, p. 36.

35. *The Capital Times*, March 1, 1945, p. 1.

36. *Ibid.*, August 8, 1945, p. 1.

37. *Congressional Record*, May 31, 1945, 79:5315 and 5320.

38. Robert M. La Follette, Jr., "A Senator Looks at Congress," *Atlantic*, Volume 172 (July, 1943), pp. 93—94.

39. *The Wisconsin State Journal*, January 29, 1946, p. 6.

40. Miles McMillin, *The Capital Times*, March 18, 1946, p. 1.

41. Fred C. Sheasby, *The Milwaukee Journal*, February 24, 1946, p. 12.

42. Interview with William R. Voigt, May 5, 1961; Confidential source.

43. Interview with Jack K. Kyle, May 8, 1961; Voigt interview.

44. Interview with Morris Rubin, May 4, 1961.

45. W. H. Lawrence, *The New York Times*, March 18, 1946, p. 1.

46. McMillin, p. 367.

47. Interview with Glenn D. Roberts, June 6, 1961.

48. *The New York Times*, March 18, 1946, p. 1.

49. Interview with Norman M. Clapp, August 2, 1961.

50. *The Capital Times*, March 18, 1946, p. 5.

51. *Ibid.*, March 18, 1946, p. 4.

52. Rex Karney, *The Wisconsin State Journal*, March 18, 1946, p. 1.

53. Interview with Gaylord Nelson, June 8, 1961.

54. Charles H. Backstrom, "The Progressive Party of Wisconsin, 1934—1946," Unpublished Ph.D. Dissertation, University of Wisconsin, 1956, p. 111.

55. Aldric Revell, *The Capital Times,* November 2, 1945, p. 2.

56. Roberts interview.

57. *The Capital Times,* April 28, 1943, p. 2.

58. *Ibid.,* August 1, 1945, p. 1.

59. Interview with A. S. Mike Monroney, August 2, 1961; Voigt interview.

60. Drew Pearson, "Merry-Go-Round," *The Capital Times,* August 21, 1946, p. 24; Clapp interview.

61. *The Capital Times,* January 26, 1946, p. 1.

62. Carey McWilliams, "The Wisconsin Riddle," *The Nation,* Volume 161 (December 15, 1945), p. 657.

63. Thomas L. Stokes, *The Wisconsin State Journal ,* March 20, 1946, p. 6.

64. *The Wisconsin State Journal,* March 18, 1946, p. 1.

65. *The Capital Times,* March 18, 1946, p. 1.

66. W. H. Lawrence, *The New York Times,* March 24, 1946, IV, p. 9.

67. *The Wisconsin State Journal,* March 18, 1946, p. 2.

CHAPTER VI

1. Quoted in Jack Anderson and Ronald W. May, *McCarthy: The Man, the Senator, the "Ism,"* (Boston, 1952), p. 53.

2. *The Capital Times,* August 13, 1944, p. 1.

3. *The Wisconsin Blue Book,* 1946, p. 595.

4. Interview with Aldric Revell, July 15, 1961.

5. Quoted in Anderson and May, pp. 78—79.

6. *The Wisconsin State Journal,* February 24, 1946, p. 6.

7. *The Capital Times,* March 24, 1946, p. 7.

8. *Ibid.,* May 3, 1946, p. 3.

9. Alfred Bowman (pseudonym), "The Man Behind McCarthy—Coleman of Wisconsin," *The Nation ,* Volume 178 (March 20, 1954), p. 236.

10. Leonard F. Schmitt to John Steinke, November 4, 1959.

11. *The Milwaukee Journal,* November 10, 1946, p. 1.

12. *The Capital Times,* May 16, 1946, p. 1.

13. Anderson and May, p. 83.
14. Interview with Ralph M. Immell, January 31, 1962.
15. *The Milwaukee Journal*, June 2, 1946, p. 12.
16. *The Capital Times*, December 23, 1945, p. 1.
17. *Ibid.*, December 9, 1945, p. 36.
18. *The Milwaukee Journal*, May 16, 1946, p. 22.
19. Leonard F. Schmitt to John Steinke, November 4, 1959.
20. *The Milwaukee Journal*, August 7, 1946, p. 18.
21. *The Capital Times*, June 30, 1946, p. 4.
22. *Ibid.*, August 8, 1946, p. 15.
23. *Ibid.*, June 13, 1946, p. 9.
24. *Ibid.*, June 16, 1946, p. 4.
25. Laurence C. Eklund, *The Milwaukee Journal*, November 10, 1946, p. 1.
26. Anderson and May, p. 101.
27. *The Capital Times*, July 16, 1946, p. 4.
28. *The Milwaukee Journal*, June 2, 1946, p. 12.
29. Quoted in Anderson and May, pp. 83—84.
30. *The Capital Times*, February 15, 1946, p. 6.
31. *Ibid.*, April 25, 1946, p. 1.
32. *Ibid.*, August 3, 1946, p. 1.
33. Howard J. McMurray to author, July 5, 1961.
34. *The Wisconsin CIO News*, July 12, 1946, p. 4.
35. *The Capital Times*, August 10, 1946, p. 7.
36. *Ibid.*, August 1, 1946, p. 7.
37. *Ibid.*, July 29, 1946, p. 7.
38. *Ibid.*, August 11, 1946, p. 12.
39. Howard J. McMurray to John Steinke, July 8, 1959.
40. *The Capital Times*, August 7, 1946, p. 6.
41. *Ibid.*
42. *Ibid.*, August 9, 1946, p. 13.
43. "McCarthy: A Documented Record," *The Progressive*, Volume 18 (April, 1954), p. 4.
44. Anderson and May, p. 104.
45. *The Capital Times*, January 31, 1952, p. 1.
46. Aldric Revell, *The Capital Times*, January 29, 1952, p. 1; see also Robert W. Ozanne, "The Effect of Communist Leadership on American Trade Unions," Unpublished Ph.D. Dissertation, the University of Wisconsin, 1954, p. 186.
47. *Congressional Record*, May 31, 1945, 79:5315—5330.

48. *The Wisconsin CIO News*, May 13, 1944, p. 1.

49. Aldric Revell to Philip F. La Follette, December 15, 1944, La Follette papers.

50. *The Wisconsin CIO News*, June 11, 1945, p. 1.

51. *Ibid.*, June 18, 1945, p. 1.

52. *Ibid.*, June 18, 1945, p. 12.

53. Herman Schendel, *The Wisconsin CIO News*, June 18, 1945, p. 12.

54. Confidential source.

55. *The Wisconsin State Journal*, June 4, 1945, p. 4.

56. *The Milwaukee Journal*, June 3, 1945, V, p. 2.

57. *Ibid.*, April 6, 1946, p. 1.

58. *The Milwaukee Labor Press*, April 11, 1946, p. 6.

59. *The Capital Times*, April 10, 1946, p. 1.

60. *Ibid.*, April 11, 1946, p. 21.

61. *The Wisconsin CIO News*, July 19, 1946, p. 4.

62. *The Capital Times*, February 22, 1946, p. 1.

63. *The Milwaukee Journal*, August 15, 1946, p. 12.

64. *Ibid.*, June 5, 1946, II, p. 1.

65. Orland S. Loomis to Robert M. La Follette, Jr., May 5, 1942, Loomis papers.

66. *The Capital Times*, June 22, 1944, p. 4.

67. *The Wisconsin CIO News*, May 17, 1946, p. 4.

68. Bobrowicz won the nomination. After the primary *The Milwaukee Journal* charged that Bobrowicz was a Communist. On that basis, the Democrats officially repudiated him. See *The Milwaukee Journal*, September 1, 1946 and subsequent issues.

69. *The Wisconsin CIO News*, August 2, 1946, p. 3.

70. Howard J. McMurray to John Steinke, July 8, 1959.

71. *The Capital Times*, June 10, 1946, p. 5.

72. Revell interview.

73. *The New York Times*, May 10, 1946, p. 1.

74. *Ibid.*, August 14, 1946, p. 16.

75. *The Capital Times*, June 5, 1946, p. 19.

76. *Ibid.*, July 23, 1946, p. 1.

77. "Special La Follette Edition," *Labor*, July 27, 1946.

78. *The Capital Times*, November 21, 1945, p. 1.

79. Photostat of entire letter in a McMurray ad, *The Capital Times*, August 11, 1946, p. 12.

80. *The Capital Times*, March 20, 1946, p. 5.

81. *Ibid.*, July 5, 1946, p. 1.

82. Leonard F. Schmitt to John Steinke, May 15, 1959.

83. *The Wisconsin CIO News*, June 14, 1946, p. 6.

84. *The Capital Times*, May 11, 1946, p. 1.

85. *The Milwaukee Journal*, August 4, 1946, II, p. 8.

86. *The Capital Times*, May 19, 1946, p. 1.

87. *Ibid.*, March 19, 1946, p. 1.

88. *Ibid.*, May 5, 1946, p. 1.

89. *The New York Times*, March 19, 1946, p. 26.

90. *The Capital Times*, July 29, 1946, p. 2.

91. *The New York Times*, July 22, 1946, p. 16.

92. *The Capital Times*, July 10, 1946, p. 1.

93. *Ibid.*, June 11, 1946, p. 1.

94. Warren Moscow, *The New York Times*, June 19, 1946, p. 24.

95. *The Capital Times*, November 10, 1940, p. 3.

96. *Ibid.*, April 1, 1946, p. 1.

97. Interview with William R. Voigt, May 5, 1961.

98. *The Capital Times*, May 19, 1946, p. 12.

99. *Ibid.*, May 20, 1946, p. 3.

100. *Ibid.*, August 3, 1946, p. 1.

101. *The New York Times*, June 9, 1946, p. 5.

102. *The Capital Times*, June 11, 1946, p. 1.

103. *Congressional Record*, March 3, 1953, 83:1501.

104. "La Follette's Defeat," *Life*, Volume 21 (August 26, 1946), pp. 26—27.

105. *Congressional Record*, March 3, 1953, 83:1498.

106. Revell interview.

107. *The Appleton Post-Crescent*, August 15, 1946, p. 16.

108. Anderson and May, p. 95.

109. Fred Sheasby, *The Milwaukee Journal*, June 23, 1946, p. 16.

110. Immell interview.

111. Interview with Glenn D. Roberts, June 6, 1961.

112. *The Capital Times*, August 11, 1946, p. 18.

113. *Ibid.*, June 16, 1946, p. 11.

114. *Ibid.*, June 4, 1946, p. 1.

115. *The Milwaukee Journal*, June 16, 1946, II, p. 1.

116. Immell interview.

117. Stanley E. Jarz to John Steinke, May 13, 1959.

118. Francis H. Wendt to John Steinke, May 14, 1959.

119. Milton R. Polland to John Steinke, May 26, 1959.

120. *The Capital Times*, August 8, 1946, p. 1.

121. Immell interview.

122. Milton R. Poland to John Steinke, May 26, 1959.

123. Stanley E. Jarz to John Steinke, May 13, 1959.

124. Bowman, p. 237.

125. *The New York Times*, August 13, 1946, p. 18.

126. *The Capital Times*, August 13, 1946, p. 5.

127. Interview with Jack K. Kyle, May 8, 1961.

128. *The Wisconsin Blue Book*, 1942, p. 661.

129. *Ibid.*, 1948, p. 604.

130. Bowman, p. 236.

131. *The Wisconsin Blue Book*, 1948, p. 604.

132. "Senator La Follette's Drive to Sell His Colleagues Modern Ways," *U. S. News* , Volume 20 (June 14, 1946), p. 70.

133. *The Appleton Post-Crescent*, August 19, 1946, p. 5.

134. Quoted in *Congressional Record*, March 3, 1953, 83: 1501—2.

135. Quoted in *Time*, Volume 61 (March 9, 1953), p. 23.

136. C. P. Trussell, *The New York Times*, August 25, 1946, IV, p. 3.

137. "La Follette's Nadir," *Newsweek*, Volume 28 (August 26, 1946), p. 17.

138. Interview with Mrs. Philip F. La Follette, July 24, 1961; interview with Norman M. Clapp, August 2, 1961.

139. *The New York Times*, August 15, 1946, p. 24.

BIBLIOGRAPHY

NEWSPAPERS

The Appleton Post-Crescent
The Capital Times (Madison)
Labor (official publication of the railroad brotherhoods in the
    United States and Canada)
The Milwaukee Journal
The Milwaukee Labor Press (A.F.L.)
The Milwaukee Sentinel
The New York Times
The Progressive
The Sheboygan Press
The Wisconsin CIO News
The Wisconsin State Journal (Madison)

MAGAZINE ARTICLES

Adamic, Louis. "La Follette Progressives Face the Future,"
    The Nation, Volume 140 (February 20, 1935), pp. 213—15.
Anderson, Paul Y. "La Follette's Bid for Power," *The Nation*,
    Volume 146 (May 7, 1938), pp. 524—25.
"Another La Follette in the Senate?" *Literary Digest*, Volume
    86 (September 26, 1925), pp. 10—11.
Bingham, Alfred M. "Revolt in the Middle West," *The Nation*,
    Volume 140 (April 3, 1935), p. 387.
Bliven, Bruce. "Robert M. La Follette," *The New Republic*,
    Volume 43 (July 1, 1925), pp. 144—45.
Bowman, Alfred. "The Man Behind McCarthy—Coleman of

Wisconsin," *The Nation,* Volume 178 (March 20, 1954), pp. 236—38. Alfred Bowman is the pseudonym of Miles McMillin of *The Capital Times.*

Brown, Francis. "La Follette: Ten Years a Senator," *Current History,* Volume 42 (August, 1935), pp. 475—80.

Brown, E. Francis. "The Progressives Make a New Bid," *Current History,* Volume 41 (November, 1934), pp. 149—54.

Byers, Mark Rhea. "A New La Follette Party," *The North American Review,* Volume 237 (May, 1934), pp. 401—9.

Cason, Clarence E. "The La Follette Succession," *The Independent,* Volume 119 (July 2, 1927), pp. 8—10.

Cook, Louis H. "Ruling Dynasty of Wisfollette," *The Saturday Evening Post,* Volume 203 (December 6, 1930), pp. 18—19.

Davenport, Walter. "Fighting Blood," *Collier's,* Volume 89 (April 23, 1932), pp. 10—11.

Davenport, Walter. "Wisconsin for Smith," *Collier's,* Volume 82 (October 20, 1928), pp. 8—9.

Davis, Elmer. "The Wisconsin Brothers," *Harper's,* Volume 178 (February, 1939), pp. 68—77.

Davis, Elmer. "Wisconsin is Different," *Harper's,* Volume 165 (October, 1932), pp. 613—24.

Devens, Stanley Price. "Wisconsin After La Follette," *The Christian Century,* Volume 56 (June 21, 1939), pp. 793—95.

Diogenes. "News and Comment from the Nation's Capital," *Literary Digest,* Volume 118 (October 13, 1934), p. 12.

Douglas, Paul H. "State Farmer-Labor Parties," *World Tomorrow,* Volume 16 (September 28, 1933), p. 544.

Evjue, William T. "'Young Bob,'" *The Nation,* Volume 176 (March 7, 1953), p. 200.

"The Fortune Survey: The La Follette Progressives," *Fortune,* Volume 18 (October, 1938), p. 90.

Frost, Stanley. "The Scramble for 'Fighting Bob's' Shoes," *The Outlook,* Volume 140 (July 29, 1925), pp. 460—62.

Giles, Barbara. "Son of Progressivism—A Portrait of 'Young Bob' La Follette," *The Outlook,* Volume 157 (April 1, 1931).

Gosnell, Harold F. and Cohen, Morris H. "Progressive Politics: Wisconsin an Example," *The American Political Science Review,* Volume 34 (October, 1940), pp. 920—35.

Groves, Harold M.   "Wisconsin's New Party," *The Nation*, Volume 139 (August 1, 1934), pp. 122—24.

Hallgren, Mauritz H.   "The New Radicalism in America,"*Contemporary Review*, Volume 142 (July, 1932), pp. 51—57.

Hallgren, Mauritz H.   "Young Bob La Follette," *The Nation*, Volume 132 (March 4, 1931), pp. 253—57.

Hopkins, Jacque and Lorraine.   "Wisconsin's Conscience: William T. Evjue," *The Nation*, Volume 181 (November 12, 1955), pp. 419—20.

"Insurgent's Way," *Time*, Volume 61 (March 9, 1953), p. 23.

Kent, Frank R.   "Little Bob Wins," *The Nation*, Volume 121 (December 30, 1925), p. 758.

La Follette, Philip F.   "The Party of Our Time: The National Progressives Organize," *Vital Speeches of the Day*, Volume 4 (May 5, 1938), pp. 450—55.

La Follette, Robert M., Jr.   "La Follette Progressivism in 1928," *Current History*, Volume 28 (June, 1928), pp. 317—19.

La Follette, Robert M., Jr.   "The Neutrality Issue," *Vital Speeches of the Day*, Volume 6 (November 1, 1939), pp. 59—61.

La Follette, Robert M., Jr.   Senate speech on anti-third term resolution, *Congressional Digest*, Volume 7 (April, 1928), pp. 124—27.

La Follette, Robert M., Jr.   "A Senator Looks at Congress," *The Atlantic*, Volume 172 (July, 1943), pp. 91—96.

"La Follette Nadir," *Newsweek*, Volume 28 (August 26, 1946), pp. 16—17.

"La Follette's Defeat," *Life*, Volume 21 (August 26, 1946), pp. 26—27.

"La Follette's Folly," *The Nation*, Volume 163 (August 24, 1946), pp. 200—201.

"La Follettes' Third Party Flag Flaps in Political Cross Winds," *Newsweek*, Volume 11 (May 9, 1938), pp. 9—10.

Lerner, Max.   "Phil La Follette—an Interview," *The Nation*, Volume 146 (May 14, 1938), pp. 552—55.

"McCarthy: A Documented Record," *The Progressive*, Volume 18 (April, 1954), entire issue.

McCoy, Donald R.   "The Formation of the Wisconsin Progressive Party in 1934," *The Historian* (Autumn, 1951), pp. 70—90.

McMillin, Miles.   "Exit the Wisconsin Progressives," *The Nation*, Volume 162 (March 30, 1946), pp. 367—68.

McMillin, Miles.   "How Taft was Saved," *The New Republic*, Volume 126 (April 14, 1952), pp. 16—17.

McMillin, Miles.   "Wisconsin—Anybody's Guess," *The Nation*, Volume 166 (April 3, 1948), pp. 372—74.

McWilliams, Carey.   "The Wisconsin Riddle," *The Nation*, Volume 161 (December 15, 1945), pp. 657—58.

Neuberger, Richard L.   "Wisconsin's Tough Old Man," *The Saturday Evening Post*, Volume 218 (February 16, 1946), pp. 9—11.

Orth, Bennington.   "The Progressive Holy Land," *The American Mercury*, Volume 18 (November, 1929), pp. 266—70.

"Paralyzed Progressives," *Collier's*, Volume 87 (March 14, 1931), p. 69.

Pringle, Henry F.   "Youth at the Top," *World's Work*, Volume 58 (May, 1929), p. 85.

"Progressives at Madison," *Time*, Volume 31 (May 9, 1938), pp. 11—13.

"Rising in the West," *Collier's*, Volume 82 (November 10, 1928), p. 35.

"Robert M. La Follette, Jr.," *Current Biography* (May, 1944), pp. 27—30.

Rodman, Selden.   "A New Radical Party," *The New Republic*, Volume 76 (September 20, 1933), pp. 151—53.

Sayre, Wallace S.   "Left Turn in Wisconsin," *The New Republic*, Volume 80 (October 24, 1934), pp. 300—302.

Schwandner, Harvey W.   "Wisconsin's Problem Governor," *The American Mercury*, Volume 48 (November, 1939), pp. 272—75.

"Senator La Follette's Drive to Sell His Colleagues Modern Ways," *U.S. News*, Volume 20 (June 14, 1946), pp. 69—70.

"Spy Profits," *Literary Digest*, Volume 123 (March 27, 1937), pp. 5—6.

Villard, Oswald Garrison.   "Issues and Men," *The Nation*, Volume 146 (May 14, 1938), p. 561.

Villard, Oswald Garrison.   "Pillars of Government: Robert M. La Follette, Jr.," *Forum & Century*, Volume 96 (August, 1936), pp. 87—91.

Williams, Howard Y.   "Minnesota Points the Way," *World To-
    morrow*, Volume 14 (March, 1931), pp. 77—79.
"Whooping it up for Hoover at Kansas City," *Literary Digest*,
    Volume 97 (June 30, 1928), pp. 38—40.
"'Young Bob,'" *The Nation*, Volume 121 (July 8, 1925), p. 59.
"'Young Bob' La Follette, Political Storm-Center," *Literary
    Digest*, Volume 118 (August 11, 1934), p. 7.

GOVERNMENT PUBLICATIONS

Congressional Record, October 29, 1941, 77:8316—25; May
    31, 1945, 79:5315—30; March 2, 1953, 83:1497—1506.
State of Wisconsin, In Supreme Court, January Term, 1934,
    Herman L. Ekern et al. vs. Theodore Dammann.
The Wisconsin Blue Book, 1927, 1931, 1933, 1935, 1940, 1942,
    1944, 1946, 1948.

BOOKS

Anderson, Jack, and May, Ronald W.   *McCarthy: The Man* ,
    The Senator, The "Ism." Boston: The Beacon Press,
    1952.
Burns, James MacGregor. *Roosevelt: The Lion and the Fox*.
    New York: Harcourt, Brace and Company, 1956.
Cole, Wayne S. *America First* . Madison: The University
    of Wisconsin Press, 1953.
Doan, Edward N. *The La Follettes and the Wisconsin Idea*.
    New York: Rinehart & Company, 1947.
Epstein, Leon D. *Politics in Wisconsin*. Madison: The Uni-
    versity of Wisconsin Press, 1958.
McCoy, Donald R. *Angry Voices* . Lawrence: University of
    Kansas Press, 1958.
Schlesinger, Arthur M., Jr.   *The Politics of Upheaval*. Bos-
    ton: Houghton Mifflin Company, 1960.
Sherwood, Robert E. *Roosevelt and Hopkins* . New York: Har-
    per & Brothers, 1950.

UNPUBLISHED WORKS

Backstrom, Charles H.   "The Progressive Party of Wisconsin, 1934—1946." Unpublished Ph.D. Dissertation, University of Wisconsin, 1956.

Kent, Alan E.   "Portrait in Isolationism: The La Follettes and Foreign Policy." Unpublished Ph.D. Dissertation, University of Wisconsin, 1956.

Meyer, Karl Ernest.   "The Politics of Loyalty: From La Follette to McCarthy in Wisconsin: 1918—1952." Unpublished Ph.D. Dissertation, Princeton University, 1956. (On microfilm at the State Historical Society of Wisconsin.)

Ozanne, Robert W.   "The Effects of Communist Leadership on American Trade Unions." Unpublished Ph.D. Dissertation, University of Wisconsin, 1954.

Steinke, John.   "The Rise of McCarthyism." Unpublished M.S. Thesis, University of Wisconsin, 1960.

DOCUMENTS

The Thomas R. Amlie papers, State Historical Society of Wisconsin.

The Henry Allen Cooper papers, State Historical Society of Wisconsin.

The Philip F. La Follette papers, State Historical Society of Wisconsin.

The Orland S. Loomis papers, State Historical Society of Wisconsin.

Philip F. La Follette, Speech for the National Progressives of America, April 28, 1938, State Historical Society of Wisconsin.

Robert M. La Follette, Jr., Speech to the Fond du Lac Convention, May 19, 1934, State Historical Society of Wisconsin.

Robert M. La Follette, Jr., Speech for the National Progressives of America, May 9, 1938, State Historical Society of Wisconsin.

"Bob's Record of Service to Wisconsin at the Nation's Capitol," (1940), State Historical Society of Wisconsin.

PERSONAL CORRESPONDENCE

Howard J. McMurray to author, July 5, 1961.

John Steinke correspondence relevant to the 1946 campaign:
Stanley E. Jarz to John Steinke, May 13, 1959.
Howard J. McMurray to John Steinke, July 8, 1959.
Milton R. Polland to John Steinke, May 26, 1959.
Leonard F. Schmitt to John Steinke, May 15, 1959; November 4, 1959.
Francis H. Wendt to John Steinke, May 14, 1959.

INTERVIEWS

Senator George Aiken, Washington, D.C., August 1, 1961, 20 minutes. United States Senator from Vermont since 1941.

Thomas R. Amlie, Madison, Wisconsin, May 4, 1961, four hours.

Justice Hugo Black, Washington, D.C., August 1, 1961, one hour. United States Senator from Alabama, 1927—1937, Associate Justice of the Supreme Court since 1937.

Norman M. Clapp, Washington, D.C., August 2, 1961, one hour, 10 minutes. Secretary to United States Senator Robert M. La Follette, Jr., 1938—1944.

William T. Evjue, Madison, Wisconsin, July 18, 1961, two hours, 5 minutes.

Ralph M. Immell, Madison, Wisconsin, January 31, 1962, two hours, 50 minutes.

Jack K. Kyle, Madison, Wisconsin, May 8, 1961, one hour, 10 minutes. Chairman of the Progressive party state central committee, 1939—1942.

Mr. and Mrs. Philip F. La Follette, Madison, Wisconsin, July 24, 1961, four hours, 5 minutes.

Miles McMillin, Madison, Wisconsin, May 26, 1961, 30 minutes.

Senator A. S. Mike Monroney, Washington, D.C., August 2, 1961, 40 minutes. United States Representative from Oklahoma, 1939—1951; United States Senator from Oklahoma since 1951.

Governor Gaylord Nelson, Madison, Wisconsin, June 8, 1961,

25 minutes. Nelson's father was chairman of the Polk County Delegation to the Portage Convention, March 17, 1946.

Maurice B. Pasch, Madison, Wisconsin, June 8, 1961; 35 minutes. Campaign manager for Orland S. Loomis in 1940 and 1942.

Aldric Revell, Madison, Wisconsin, July 15, 1961, two hours.

Glenn D. Roberts, Madison, Wisconsin, June 6, 1961, 50 minutes. Chairman of the Progressive party state central committee, 1942—1946.

Morris H. Rubin, Madison, Wisconsin, May 4, 1961, one hour, 10 minutes. Editor of the *Progressive* since 1940.

William R. Voigt, Madison, Wisconsin, May 5, 1961, one hour, 15 minutes. Staff assistant to Senator Robert M. La Follette, Jr. on the Senate Finance Committee, 1939—1941; personal assistant to Senator La Follette, 1943—1947.

INDEX